THEotherAMERICA

GANGS

by
Gail B. Stewart

Photographs by
Natasha Frost

Lucent Books, P.O. Box 289011, San Diego, CA 92198-9011

These and other titles are included in *The Other America* series:

Battered Women	Illegal Immigrants
The Elderly	People with AIDS
Gangs	Teen Mothers
Gay and Lesbian Youth	Teen Runaways
The Homeless	Teens in Prison

Cover design: Carl Franzen

Library of Congress Cataloging-in-Publication Data

Stewart, Gail, 1949–
　　Gangs / by Gail B. Stewart; photographs by Natasha Frost.
　　　　p. cm.— (The other America)
　　Includes bibliographical references and index.
　　Summary: Background information on the history of gangs in America precedes first-person accounts by four gang members from different backgrounds and with differing ideas about the role of gangs in their lives.
　　ISBN 1-56006-340-8　　(alk. paper)
　　1. Gangs—United States—Juvenile literature.　2. Gang members—United States—Interviews—Juvenile literature.　[1. Gangs.　2. Gang members—interviews.]　I. Frost, Natasha, ill.　II.Title.　III. Series: Stewart, Gail, 1949–　　Other America.
HV6439.U5S77　　1997
364.1′06′6—dc20　　　　　　　　　　　　　　　　　96–36697
　　　　　　　　　　　　　　　　　　　　　　　　　　CIP
　　　　　　　　　　　　　　　　　　　　　　　　　　AC

Printed in the U.S.A.
Copyright © 1997 by Lucent Books, Inc.
P.O. Box 289011, San Diego, CA 92198-9011

Contents

Foreword

O, YES,
I SAY IT PLAIN,
AMERICA NEVER WAS AMERICA TO ME.
AND YET I SWEAR THIS OATH—
AMERICA WILL BE!
> LANGSTON HUGHES

Perhaps more than any other nation in the world, the United States represents an ideal to many people. The ideal of equality— of opportunity, of legal rights, of protection against discrimination and oppression. To a certain extent, this image has proven accurate. But beneath this ideal lies a less idealistic fact—many segments of our society do not feel included in this vision of America.

They are the outsiders—the homeless, the elderly, people with AIDS, teenage mothers, gang members, prisoners, and countless others. When politicians and the media discuss society's ills, the members of these groups are defined as what's wrong with America; they are the people who need fixing, who need help, or increasingly, who need to take more responsibility. And as these people become society's fix-it problem, they lose all identity as individuals and become part of an anonymous group. In the media and in our minds these groups are identified by condition—a disease, crime, morality, poverty. Their condition becomes their identity, and once this occurs, in the eyes of society, they lose their humanity.

The Other America series reveals the members of these groups as individuals. Through in-depth interviews, each person tells his or her unique story. At times these stories are painful, revealing individuals who are struggling to maintain their integrity, their humanity, their lives, in the face of fear, loss, and economic and spiritual hardship. At other times, their tales are exasperating,

4

demonstrating a litany of poor choices, shortsighted thinking, and self-gratification. Nevertheless, their identities remain distinct, their personalities diverse.

As we listen to the people of *The Other America* series describe their experiences they cease to be stereotypically defined and become tangible, individual. In the process, we may begin to understand more profoundly and think more critically about society's problems. When politicians debate, for example, whether the homeless problem is due to a poor economy or lack of initiative, it will help to read the words of the homeless. Perhaps then we can see the issue more clearly. The family who finds itself temporarily homeless because it has always been one paycheck from poverty is not the same as the mother of six who has been chronically chemically dependent. These people's circumstances are not all of one kind, and perhaps we, after all, are not so very different from them. Before we can act to solve the problems of the Other America, we must be willing to look down their path, to see their faces. And perhaps in doing so, we may find a piece of ourselves as well.

Introduction

"It happened so fast, we didn't even know for sure what it was," the eleven-year-old Chicago girl says. "We were standing outside our building, talking to some neighbors. My dad had just bought us ice cream bars from the store down on the corner, because it was my sister Kimberly's birthday. Kimberly was two years old, too young to have a party, so my dad promised her ice cream.

"So anyway, we were talking and stuff with these people who live in our building, too. It was a hot evening, so lots of people were outside. And all of a sudden this old orange car filled with gangbangers drives up and we all look. And then there were explosions and shots, and the people in the car were shooting—not toward us, but toward the other side of the street. The other people across the street were shooting back at them, too.

"Everybody was screaming and diving out of the way until the shooting stopped and the car screeched away. My father had jumped on me, told me to get down, but then he let me up. And my mom started screaming, 'She's dead! My baby is dead!' She was holding my baby sister; Kimberly had got shot by them gangbangers. She had blood and ice cream all over her. And even when the police came and the ambulance took Kimberly away, there was still blood and ice cream on the steps of our building."

WAR ZONES

The tragedy described by eleven-year-old Lara occurred on Chicago's South Side in the summer of 1994, but it could have happened in any American city. The little girl who was killed was the victim of gang violence. She was hit by a bullet from a gang member's gun—a bullet that was intended for someone else.

Gangs, and the violence that accompanies them, have become

synonymous with life in cities like New York and Los Angeles. However, law enforcement officials say that gang activity is no longer limited to the largest cities in America.

"Gangs can be found anywhere these days," says one official. "A lot of the gangs used to be concentrated in Los Angeles. That was where some of the large gangs like the Bloods and the Crips started way back when. But now we see them in smaller cities and towns, rural areas, even Indian reservations."

The statistics are staggering: in 1995 more than thirteen hundred of America's cities and towns reported evidence of gang activity, from graffiti painted on alleys, bridges, and city buses to drive-by shootings and murder. Some cities say that perhaps 70 percent of their murders are gang related; others put that figure even higher.

"We can't keep up," says one Chicago counselor who has worked with youths in gangs. "In some neighborhoods we've got 80 percent of the boys between ten and fifteen already claiming a gang. We can't even make a dent in the numbers. The schools in our town have become battlegrounds, and the streets are war zones, with innocent people being held hostage. Kids are killing each other at an astonishing rate, yet we can't seem to do anything to stop it."

No one seems to know exactly how many gangs or gang members there are in America. In 1992 U.S. police departments estimated that there were about five thousand gangs, with a membership of about one million. Today many experts say they'd double that figure.

"It's hard to really know," says one police officer in a gang unit. "The number of gangs keeps changing because new ones keep splintering off the old ones. You got Crips, but you also got a bunch of sets [subgroups within a gang] like Shotgun Crips and Four-Seven Crips. And you got Vice Lords, but you got Four-Corner Lords, Insane Vice Lords, Trey-Eight Vice Lords, and whatever else they've started this week. And as soon as a set starts, you got kids jumping in, left and right. There's no shortage of kids who join, that's for sure."

FROM THE DEAD RABBITS AND STRIKEBREAKERS . . .

While it is true that America's teens and preteens are joining gangs in unprecedented numbers and that the body counts are rising at record rates, it is also true that gangs in American cities are not new. Gangs have been creating problems for cities since the nineteenth century.

Irish immigrants made up most of the first gangs and had names like the Plug Uglies and the Dead Rabbits. (The Dead Rabbits were so named because, as they advanced into battle with other gangs, they held up poles with the bodies of dead rabbits jammed onto them.) These gangs fought with one another for territory and, in addition, beat up and stole from shopkeepers and pedestrians in the area.

During the early years of the twentieth century, the number of gangs increased, as did the number of European immigrants. Rough gangs roamed the poorer neighborhoods of New York City, fighting one another with stones, bricks, knives, and brass knuckles.

While most of this early gang violence was sparked because of turf wars, the early 1900s saw another reason for gang violence: the unions. Union leaders began hiring gang members to murder and beat up strikebreakers as early as 1911. It did not take long for factory owners to respond in kind; they hired their own gangs to fight the unions.

. . . To the Crips and Bloods

There were few black gangs in the early 1900s. Most gang members in New York and other large cities were European immigrants who used gang activity either as protection in rough neighborhoods or as a way to engage in crime.

However, as more and more African Americans moved north to work in factories during the years of World War I, the composition of gangs changed, too. A lack of opportunity for blacks, both in employment and in education, seemed to cause more black youths to seek out gang activity. By the mid-1940s there were gangs made up of black youths in cities such as New York, Chicago, Los Angeles, and Detroit. In the 1940s the Vice Lords, one of the largest Chicago gangs, was formed in St. Charles, Illinois, at the Illinois State Training School for Boys. As these boys were released from this reform school and sent back to their neighborhoods in Chicago, they soon became an intimidating force.

On the West Coast, gang activity was growing, too. Sometime between the late 1960s and early 1970s, the Crips were formed in Los Angeles at Washington High School. They adopted blue as their color, since it was one of the school's colors, and soon became the most feared gang in that city.

"They were the most violent gang anyone had seen," says one Los Angeles investigator. "They organized their members to commit crimes ranging from extortion, assault, robbery—you name it—all the way up to murder. Their rivals, of course, were and still are the Bloods, originally called Piru, from the name of the street where the leaders lived. This was the beginning of a nightmare for us in law enforcement—big, new gangs who were armed to the teeth. And it's getting worse with every passing year."

Gang violence has escalated in the years since the first gangs roamed the neighborhoods of New York City, as automatic and semiautomatic weapons have replaced brass knuckles and switchblades. Changed, too, are the ways gangs make money.

Gangs today control a large share of the drug market, the same way in which the Mafia controlled the trade in liquor during the days of Prohibition. As crack cocaine has become the drug of choice in the bleakest neighborhoods of the city, gangs have become distributors.

"On any city block, in any bar or pool hall, any of the apartment buildings and projects in the inner city, there are the sellers," says one youth counselor. "The kids can be as young as nine or ten; all they have to do is hand over a little bag and hold on to the money. Every hour or so an overseer comes and takes the money, makes sure the dealer has more crack to sell if he needs it, and the whole thing starts over again."

There seems to be no limit to the amount of money to be made in the selling and distribution of drugs, primarily because the supply of customers is endless. In 1994 the Gangster Disciple gang in Chicago made an estimated five hundred million dollars from selling drugs. California investigators say that the Bloods and Crips together have cornered more than 35 percent of the national crack market.

VIOLENCE OUT OF CONTROL

As gangs in the United States have grown financially, the level of violence they produce has grown also. Today's gangs baffle older drug dealers, some of whom were active in the days of the most notorious Mafia criminals.

"Bring back the Mob [the Mafia] any day," says one law enforcement official from California. "These new kids scare the dickens out of me. They have no regard for life or family; there is no honor. The Mob was violent, of course, but had respect for a man's family. A fellow cheated on them, maybe kept some of the drugs himself? They'd kill him, sure. But never his family. These gangs we have now settle scores by shooting a guy's wife and baby."

Even gang leaders from ten years ago seem bewildered when they talk about the level of indiscriminate violence today. "Even back in the early 1980s you wouldn't see these little kids being killed, all this cross-fire stuff," says one former gang member. "If you were going to waste somebody, you'd waste him. It wouldn't be the neighbors that would get killed. It's kind of scary now. It's like some of these boys would just as soon blow you away as look at you twice."

Some experts see the increased violence as a result of the drug trade. They point to the fierce competition for territory among drug dealers, where the income from a single city block can make a huge difference in profits.

"You got area coordinators, regents, and enforcers in the chain of command," says one former gang member. "I mean, this is all organized like some Wall Street corporation. And somebody gets their part of the territory stolen or one of the shorties [young drug dealers] gets jumped by another gang and loses his stash of money—you got a war on your hands."

A NEW KIND OF THINKING

While the big-money stakes certainly add to the gang violence, drug-related issues are not the main cause of the killings and shootings today. More and more, say counselors and youth workers, the violence is triggered by trivial things.

"Sometimes it's the fact that somebody pushed somebody else, maybe by mistake," says one Detroit counselor. "Or somebody is wearing the wrong color bandanna or made the wrong sign—hand signal—in the wrong neighborhood. That's got nothing to do with drugs. That's just trivial nonsense, but it results in death. Don't believe me? In Chicago last summer a gang war broke out in one of the projects, and over three days thirteen people were killed. The reason? Somebody was going out with a girl someone else wanted to go out with!"

One member of the Eight-Trey Crips serving a life sentence for murder agrees, recalling that one of the biggest wars within his gang was because of a leather coat that one teen stole from another. The violence resulted in the deaths of twenty-six people.

If, indeed, young people in gangs are shooting people for increasingly far-fetched reasons, they certainly have more sophisticated weapons with which to do so. While a decade ago a gang member considered himself well armed with a sawed-off shotgun, today's gangbangers have whole arsenals at their disposal: AK-47s, Uzis, street sweepers, and Tech-9s. In addition to being fast and powerful, these weapons can spray bullets that kill dozens of people with a single squeeze of the trigger.

"Today, you got an argument with a guy who made you mad on the bus?" says one counselor. "You don't punch him in the nose. You get your strap [gun] and you take him out. The thinking isn't very sophisticated; the reasons aren't very new. It's just the way the fight takes place that's changed."

WHO ARE THESE KIDS?

As people grapple to understand the violence and mayhem that gangs produce, they also seek answers. Who are the young people who join gangs? If, as one gang member suggests, there are only three futures available for kids in gangs—"a tomb, a cell, or a drug box [coffin]"—why would being part of a gang appeal to anyone?

For some it's an easy way to make money or gain prestige. For a lot of young people gangs represent safety in neighborhoods that are definitely unsafe. But those who work with young people in gangs say that there are far deeper reasons than these.

One reason is very clear to those who have worked with young people in gangs: security. In a time when, as many people believe, most of our culture's institutions—church, family, school—have crumbled, the gang remains a powerful force. "Within the gang you're somebody," one gang counselor observes. "People respect you; you've got a name. Most of the kids I see are from one-parent or no-parent families. Nobody notices them, nobody really cares about them, and nobody has time for them. But the gang has time for them; their 'homies' have time. Sometimes it's as simple as that."

The four young people interviewed in *The Other America: Gangs* are members of different gangs. They come from different backgrounds and have differing ideas about the role of the gang in their lives.

Tajan is a sixteen-year-old who is a proud member of the Gangster Disciples. He is intelligent and wishes people would get to know him before passing judgment.

Edwin, who is originally from El Salvador, is also sixteen. Although most of his best friends are in the Latin Kings gang, he is still making up his mind whether he wants to be jumped in; that is, made an official gang member through an initiation process that is usually violent. He has seen a lot of violence firsthand, both in El Salvador and with his Latin King friends.

Twenty-year-old Kim is a Vice Lord. She is the mother of a young son, whom she dresses in gang colors. She has had close family members killed in drive-by shootings.

Dewayne, eighteen, is blind. His eyes were shot out by a fellow Crip almost two years ago. Although he still considers himself close to the people in his set, or gang subgroup, Dewayne speaks with bitterness about the realities of gang life. He says that he told his younger brothers, "You ain't never going to be in a gang—not while I'm breathing."

Tajan

"PEOPLE THINK WE'RE ALL BAD,
LIKE WE'RE NOT WORTH ANYTHING
BECAUSE WE'RE [IN A GANG]. BUT
THE WAY I THINK IS THAT YOU
CAN'T JUDGE SOMETHING YOU
DON'T KNOW ANYTHING ABOUT."

As he watches the visitor walk up the uneven concrete walkway to his front porch, the teenage boy appears casual, almost bored. He makes his best attempt at an indifferent nod and leads the way inside the house. He sits down in an oversized chair that faces a television and indicates that his visitor can sit on a sofa that faces in the same general direction.

"Bulls are playing Orlando," he mutters. "My boy Shaq is going to beat the you know what out of Jordan. Jordan is having a bad day, but that don't bother me one bit."

"LOOKING OUT FOR MY OWN"

His name is Tajan, and he is sixteen. He lives in this struggling neighborhood along the north edge of the city, where the gangs and violence that are always nearby are becoming more and more noticeable. Like countless other boys in the neighborhood, he dresses in what is almost a uniform among them: baggy pants, oversized shirt, and a bandanna around his head—in Tajan's case, a blue one. He is, he says, a GD, a member of the Gangster Disciples.

He lives with his mother, a pretty, partially sighted woman in her thirties, and a houseful of younger brothers and sisters. When he finally gets around to smiling, his face looks younger than sixteen. Smiles, however, seem rare for Tajan.

"I've been living here a pretty long time," he says. "My dad? You mean my real dad? I don't know much about him. He left when I was, like, two or three and went back to where he was from. Someplace in Ohio, I think. He came back when I was about thirteen, trying to be all in my life and whatever, but I had no time for him. I was busy. I got to take care of my own business."

This final statement is spoken solemnly, and he pauses a moment, thinking.

"I don't really know what the deal is with my mom now. I got a stepdad, her little husband and whatever," he drawls, rolling his eyes. "I don't know what their deal is, though, if they're, like, separated or divorced. He stops through and stuff, because these little kids here, they're his and everything. I don't pay much attention. I am just busy looking out for my own, for myself, you know? That's what I'm doing these days."

"I Was Always the Athletic Type, Winning Trophies . . . and Stuff"

Although his involvement with the GDs is a big part of his life now, Tajan admits that in years past running with a gang would have been the last thing he would have envisioned for himself.

"If you were to talk to me back a few years ago, like, when I was twelve, thirteen, I would have told you I was going to be, like, a professional athlete," he says with a hint of a smile. "I was always the athletic type, you know, winning trophies, ribbons, lots of medals, and stuff."

His voice suddenly becomes more animated, the relaxed drawl disappearing momentarily.

"You see in there, look over by the mantel," he says proudly, pointing at a cluster of silver and gold trophies over the fireplace in the next room. "Those are all my trophies. And see over here, in this room? Those are all mine. I got them all over the place, you know what I'm saying? Baseball, basketball, hockey. I got medals in hockey, too. They're in my room. Soccer. I even got medals in tennis. We started running out of places to put all this stuff.

"I got in trouble starting in about junior high, and I kind of stopped doing sports. I had to go stay with my grandmother because of some trouble I got in. And I tried to get in some teams up there, but man, that's so expensive there, as compared to here in the city. It's, like, a thousand dollars a season for hockey to get on a good traveling team or whatever up there. No way I could do that."

He settles back in the chair, his excitement slowly evaporating. "So I just got off sports. It just happened. It wasn't how I wanted it, but it just turned out that way. You ask me why I don't get back into it; I mean, I'm home now, right? But see, it's been three years since I was on a team. I wouldn't be able to start, and it's not fun sitting on the bench.

"I still play some basketball, just pickup games at the park or whatever. But see, now if you play, you play for your high school. I don't think I could just walk in and make no varsity team, not after being out of it for three years. And I don't want to just play in no recreational league or through the parks. There ain't no competition there. Plus, all those games end up in people fighting each other. I want to play for championships. That's the kind of competition that's really exciting."

Tajan says that besides being good in sports, he was also good in school when he was younger.

Although he lives with his mother and several brothers and sisters, Tajan says he doesn't have much time for his family these days. "I am just busy looking out for my own, for myself, you know?"

"It wasn't all A's, but I maintained real good," he says. "I really liked geography best. Hey, I even won a trophy for that, too. I'm more into stuff like geography, I guess, because it seems pretty real to me. I can explain things because I've seen a lot of things. I've traveled a lot, and I remember what I saw along the way.

"I've been in every state west of here, so I know things. I mean, you can ask me a question about Wyoming, and that wouldn't be hard for me, since I've been there."

He pauses, almost as though he really wants to be quizzed about Wyoming.

"The reason I traveled, I guess, started out for good reasons, with my grandma. She's cool, yeah. I've always been close to her. She and I did lots of traveling together. See, when I was younger, she'd, like, be proud of me for doing good in sports and in school. She took me on a trip to California, just me and her. We drove there, all the way. We saw a lot of stuff, took the time to look at things, explore around. That was really nice; that was a good memory. That was during the school year, too—a little break, since I was doing good."

Tajan shifts position in his chair, glancing up a moment at the television.

"She's probably the person I was closest to in our family. I like her a lot. I get along okay with my stepsisters, too, but I don't hang around here much. I don't really care, I guess. Most of the time I just try not to be here, around all these kids."

He glares at one of the children, a boy of about four.

"I wouldn't be here even now, except you're here, asking me all these questions."

BAD ATTITUDE

Tajan says that he started getting into trouble when he was about twelve. It was then that he began disliking school and becoming what he admits was something of a disruption.

"I was always getting suspended," he says. "Fighting on the bus, fighting at recess, fighting at lunch. I don't know, all the kids around here liked to fight. Me, I don't really like it, but I won't back out or nothing. I don't really think I'm a violent person or whatever. I think I was just kind of easy to get in a fight with.

"A lot of it was my teachers. Man, they got me in such a bad mood that they got my attitude going. I guess the bottom line is they worked my nerves, the way they acted. Made me so mad that I felt like fighting, I guess. Like this one teacher, Miss Brennan. She had this attitude that she was always right just because she was a teacher.

"One time she was wrong. She said something in class I *knew* wasn't right, and I said so. I can't remember what the subject was, but I even told her what the right answer was, since I knew it. But she just got so pissed off, so mad. She took me out in the hall, told me she never wanted me to embarrass her in front of the class ever again."

Tajan looks disgusted, remembering.

"I got in an argument. Cussed her out. I got sent down to the office. Got suspended for that one. It was just plain stupid, her not even being able to handle not being right all the time. And fine, so maybe I lost my temper, but she had it coming, the way I see it."

Besides being incapable of admitting their errors, Tajan says, some of the teachers prejudged him, which angered him even more.

"They'd tell other teachers I'd never even had before that I was a smart aleck, or whatever," he says. "Then it's, like, they think they already know me, and they've judged me even before I open my mouth. That's what I hate more than anything. Or people who accuse me of something when I didn't do it. Man, that's something that doesn't work for me. And that was happening all the time, it seems like."

FIGHTING

Tajan maintains that his grades reflected his souring attitude toward his teachers. Instead of A's and B's, he began getting D's and incompletes, which affected his eligibility to play sports.

"I wasn't doing good in school, so I couldn't play sports," he remembers. "It seemed like there wasn't anything much to look forward to in the day, you know? Like, before, I'd know that there was a game or even a practice or something after school or after dinner. That would make the day go faster, something good coming up that I liked. But that ended. So . . . ."

It was during this time that he started getting into fights at school—at recess, at lunch, on the bus. It didn't seem to matter, says Tajan; he'd find a fight no matter where he was.

"I don't think it was because I was violent or anything," he explains. "I didn't even really like to fight. I won't back out or nothing, but I don't remember going looking for a fight. It's just that all the kids around here like to fight. And I was easy to get in a fight with. I guess I was just in that kind of mood. I'd get suspended, get sent home for a while. Then I'd go back to school, and it would happen again. My mom was getting tired of it. She told me she was trying to be understanding, but she couldn't figure out why I was always in the middle of something."

ASSAULT

The real trouble occurred because of a fight. Tajan was involved in what would have been an assault charge if the police had caught him.

"I was down at the park with a couple of my friends," he says. "I don't know all of what happened, but there was this kid up there who was talking all this neck, you know? Neck—it's like talking trash, talking about your family, your mom, just saying stuff, getting loud at the mouth.

Because of his constant fighting, Tajan was sent to live with his grandmother. Tajan says, "I kind of wanted to get away from here because, truthfully, I was getting kind of tired of the fighting, too."

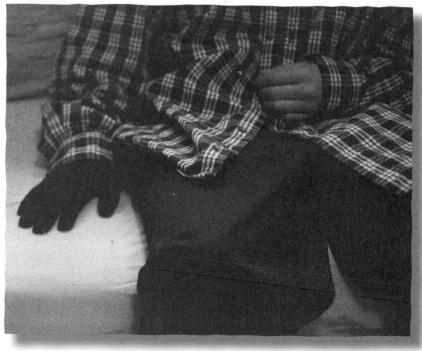

"Anyway, that was going on, and I started fighting with him. I was beating him down—by the playground, over by the swings there. And this one dude was, like, 'I'm going to call the cops for what you're doing to him.' The guy I was fighting, I knew him. He used to be in one of my classes, just a kid looking for a fight I guess."

Tajan looks amused. "I guess he came looking in the right place. He was down on the ground! My cousin Mark ran over, and he's, like, going through the guy's pockets, taking money out and everything. And you should have seen it. After I was done beating that dude down, all the little kids in the park came over there and started taking everything else. I mean it—his shoes, his jacket, everything. I'm telling you, it was kind of funny."

What was *not* so funny, he says, was his mother's reaction to this latest fight.

"She was real mad," he admits. "I mean, you might as well say I got away with it as far as the police were concerned. They never caught me. But when I got home and my mom found out about the fight, she was in a rage. She told me I was getting in too many fights, and this was the last straw. She sent me away from home, told me to go live with my grandma."

Did being sent away hurt his feelings? Tajan shakes his head.

"Naw, I didn't mind. I kind of wanted to get away from here because, truthfully, I was getting kind of tired of the fighting, too. I wanted to go to a different school, away from the city a little bit."

"ONE THING WAS REALLY BUGGING ME, THOUGH"

He remained with his grandmother for almost three years. He says that for the most part he enjoyed the time away.

"I did good in school there," he brags. "My teachers loved me. There was a fight the first day on the bus. Some kid called me a nigger. But after that, everything was cool. I just kind of had to show everybody that I was not somebody who would tolerate that, you know what I'm saying? And I showed them. I mean, that kid ended up being a friend of mine, and I had lots of other friends there, too."

Tajan says that the only thing he did miss while staying with his grandmother was the diversity of the city.

"One thing was really bugging me, though. It was that everybody was white," he says. "I couldn't stand being around all those white people all the time. I mean, I'm part black, part white; I just wanted to see lots of different kinds of people.

"Look here," he says, pointing outside to his front porch where four of his friends are hanging around talking. "There's not just black kids, not just white kids. I got lots of friends, all kinds. I'm a city person. I'm used to differences. And at my grandma's, there weren't too many, you know what I'm saying?"

GROWTH AND DEVELOPMENT

It was partly this need to touch base with his city friends, he says, that led to his interest in joining the Gangster Disciples.

"I would come home on weekends once in a while, just for visits," he remembers. "Sometimes I even skipped school and came back to the city just to visit people. Back and forth, you know, seeing two sets of friends. It was like being in a divorced family.

"And when I'd come back here, I'd be just kicking with my friends, and it seemed like they were all of a sudden really into gang stuff. They gave me some papers [about the Gangster Disciples] to read. Said they wanted to know what I thought about it. I mean, they weren't making me do anything. They said, 'We're not asking you; this should be on you, not a forced thing.'"

Tajan says that he was impressed with what he learned about the GDs.

"It's not all that stuff you read about in the newspapers. It really isn't," he maintains. "It's not all gangbanging and stuff like that. To me, GD could stand for Growth and Development. It's more like an organization. See, the GDs was started by a Black Panther in Chicago named Larry Hoover. That's what the stuff was that I read, like, five or six pages' worth, explaining it all. It started out as the BOSs, the Brothers of the Struggle. I mean, from that, you can kind of tell what his beliefs are. It's, like, we're here to help out the neighborhood. We're more into protecting than anything. It's a pride thing, pride and loyalty to the neighborhood where you live."

But what does that mean? Do GDs then refuse to participate in the shootings and other violent activity that has become the symbol of gangs in America's cities? Tajan snorts.

"Not at all. Hey, we aren't afraid of whatever. Life can get down to other things. It can be drive-bys, shootings, fighting, stuff like that. Stuff pops up, you know, and we gotta get dirty sometimes. But it's not all about that. That's the thing people have to remember."

THE LAW OF THE IGNORANT OUTBURST

Tajan feels that the GDs are unjustly lumped in with more violent gangs, those without the ideals that he claims his gang represents. He knows that there are many gangs in the city, with new ones being formed all the time. It is easy to understand, he says, why people think that all gangs are the same.

"Sure, there are stereotypes," he says. "I mean, even among the GDs there are people who want to stress the Gangster Disciple part of it. I mean, there are so many gangs around here, it's hard to re-member what they all stand for. I mean, just around this part of town, there are GDs, Blackstones, DarkSkins, Light Skins, Shorty Mags, Latin Kings, Bloods, Crips . . . it goes on and on. But the thing is, the GDs are pretty cool with everybody, unless there's a reason not to be.

Tajan insists that gangs aren't solely about violence; instead, he says, they're more about "pride and loyalty to the neighborhood."

"See, in our gang there's this law called the Ignorant Outburst. It means if I see somebody from another gang walking down the street, let's say, and I decide to go over and start tripping on [fighting with] him, I'd be guilty of an ignorant outburst. I'm not supposed to do that just for no reason. I mean, there are some gangs that will do that—might shoot at a person because he's got the wrong color on or something. But with GDs it's supposed to be different."

If he commits an ignorant outburst, Tajan says that his fellow gang members can take immediate, and painful, action.

"It can mean a mouth shot—getting hit in the face by someone in my own gang," he explains. "But the difference here is . . . let's say he's walking down the street and he has something to say to me, starts saying something bad to me. Then we can get dirty. That's the difference. I won't take none of that stuff from nobody. No self-respecting GD will."

COLORS AND SIGNS

What about colors? Does he have to be sure he's wearing his gang's colors each day? Tajan makes a face.

"Nah," he says. "Look here." He calls out the screen door, where four other teens in baggy pants and shirts sit smoking and talking quietly.

"You see these men here? They ain't got no colors the same, right? Nothing that binds them, as you can see. We don't need that stuff, like Bloods and Crips. I mean, some GDs represent themselves by wearing blue and black, but it's not like you have to."

Signs are a different story, he says. The GD sign, a hand signal that resembles a pitchfork, is considered important by gang members. For someone from another gang to intentionally throw, or display, the sign incorrectly is a high insult.

"It happens all the time, that stuff," Tajan says. "I'll be standing outside when a bus goes by my house, and some kid will be looking out the window and see me. He might hit me up [make the GD sign] or else throw me down—you know, do it upside down or something like that. Now, to some guys throwing a sign down is a good reason to shoot someone. Me, I don't trip on that. I just ignore it. There's more important things, you know. You got to choose your battles.

As a member of the Gangster Disciples, Tajan often wears his gang's colors, along with baggy pants, an oversized shirt, and a bandanna.

"Like, there was this guy that got worked over by some gang. I don't know which one. He was a deaf guy, right? He couldn't talk except with sign language. And he's getting on a bus, using sign language, and some gangbangers think he's throwing down their sign. So they gouge his eyes out or something."

He looks disgusted. "Man, I can't quite figure the intelligence of that, you know? Some dumb boys, I guess. I mean, how hard is it to tell the difference between sign language and somebody disrespecting you?

"I know for GDs that the pitchfork-up sign is the same everywhere—in Chicago, whatever. I don't know about these new little GDs coming around, doing their own little thing. You know, starting their own little gangs, like splinter groups or whatever. Dog Pound Gangstas, South Side Disciples, whatever. I don't know and, really, I don't care. I don't want to involve myself with people I'm not really close to. They can do what they want, I guess."

He nods his head back toward his friends on the front porch. "I just know what GD is for me, for my boys."

No Problem with the Little Guys

When he first became part of the GDs, Tajan was only in the city part-time, since he was spending most of his time with his grandmother. Even so, he says, he was able to represent his gang in that suburban school as well.

"It's funny," he says, "how many of the new kids to the school were in gangs, too. Lots of them had transferred from city schools and brought a lot of that stuff with them.

"There were these guys out there that started a little something with me at the school. They called themselves AGDs. They were talking some stuff to me at school, stuff like that. So I grabbed a couple of my boys here, and I showed them that I wasn't going to take no more of that. We fought at a park—a straight-up fight, no guns involved. But no problem for us. They just thought they were hard, but they weren't. Most people don't even bother to fight us. I mean, some just ignore us. The jocks, the big-time druggies, they just are into their own little thing. The rest of them . . . they just go their own way and hope to God they don't get messed with."

Living the Life

So exactly what is involved in being in a gang? Is it more than just signs and handshakes, more than fighting?

"It's not just the people you see, you know," he explains. "I mean, for the GDs, we're an organization. I think that's true with most gangs, but I don't know for sure. There are functions where everybody meets up twice a week. For us, it's Thursdays and Sundays, every week.

"The word gets out, gets passed around. The place is always different because—think about it—you don't want everybody knowing where they'll be able to find all the GDs around here in one place. That's hazardous. So it changes; the place is always different. Like, for this next Thursday, someone told me it's going to be in the park down about a mile from here, at 5:00. Or next time it might be at someone's apartment or in an alley, or whatever."

The meetings are run, he says, by leaders, the same as with meetings in any organization.

"There's area coordinators, regionals, governors," he says. "Who's in charge is figured out by seniority mostly. They're called OGs, original gangsters. Most of those dudes are pretty old—in their thirties, I guess.

"At the meetings there's all kinds of stuff that might go on. Maybe there's trouble with another gang, maybe a war starting up. Maybe they'll be asking everybody if they know how to get more guns. Or else maybe there's some news, like someone getting shot or jumped, or whatever. That is how wars start, someone getting jumped or shot at. That happened to my cousin. He got shot five times, and it started a war.

"Sometimes it's someone getting jumped into the gang, you know. It's, like, making it official. They usually get beat on for a bit to make sure they're tough enough to take it. Or if it's a girl and she wants to be an SOS, a Sister of the Street, then she can either get jumped in, or . . . ."

His voice trails off, and he laughs with embarrassment. "They can, uh, well, they can have sex with every dude. That's the other way for females to get into the gang."

Tajan maintains that not all gang members carry pistols, but it is important to know how to get one if the situation demands it. What would such a situation be?

"Well, if someone is shooting at me, I can't think of a reason not to shoot back," he says with a shrug. "I, myself, don't have a gun, but I have access to one, or more than one, if need be. My mom, she knows I'd use a gun, sure. But she knows I'm not stupid; I'm not going to start taking people on for showing down pitchforks, like I said before.

"I think if you're not carrying a gun, a razor blade is what you want. That you should always have. You can hide it, then just put it between your fingers, and you got yourself some protection."

"I Feel Like I'm Ready, I'm Protected"

He pulls a stretchy black cotton glove out of his pocket. "I carry one of these, too. Called a suicide glove. All it is is another way of protecting yourself. See, if I'm looking at someone's pistol, maybe thinking of buying it or just checking it out, I don't want to leave no prints. So that's important. Also if you're handling ammunition. I mean, shell casings can have prints on them, same as a gun. But some people are so stupid they don't know it and load their guns without using a glove. Not me. I feel like I'm ready, I'm protected."

And being protected, taking precautions, is an important thing when violence seems to be lurking around every corner, he says.

"I think the biggest thing is being smart, being careful. You gotta keep your eyes open, watch for things that don't feel right. Like, one time I was with some of my friends, and we were just down the street here, down by the little store there on the corner. And I'm watching this bunch of boys, these Crips, hanging around. Lots of them, just in front of the store.

"And I say to my boys, 'Are you seeing this? Tell me this doesn't look strange to you.' And then all of a sudden, while we were just hanging back, watching, here comes a car and—BOOM-BOOM-BOOM!—somebody starts shooting at them. They all duck inside the store. I figure they got set up or else they were getting ready to start tripping themselves. And if I hadn't been looking, me and my boys, we could have been right in the middle of that and not been so lucky, right?"

He acknowledges that there have been times when he hasn't been so observant and that his negligence might have resulted in injury, or worse.

"Me and a couple of friends, we were just riding down the street on our bikes, you know, and these kids are saying, like, 'G-D-K, G-D-K [GD Killer]!' And we got down off our bikes and we're getting ready to scrap. Two of them, four of us. And if I'd been smarter, I might have wondered why they're going to take four of us on if they got no backup. But there was nobody around that I could see, so I figured we were cool.

"So we were doing a little fighting, just punching, shoving, and this one dude says, 'To hell with this.' Because we were outnumbering them, you know. Then he says, 'Let me get the strap.' So he goes over to his boy, and his homie throws him a gun. I didn't even know they had one. And so the dude just popped in the clip—SNAP. And then he shot one in the air—BOOM! And BOOM-BOOM-BOOM-BOOM-BOOM! Five of them, just like that, right at us. It was so close, man. I could hear those bullets whizzing by.

"You can sometimes avoid stuff like that by being careful. But sometimes not." Tajan shrugs. "Like I said, it's dangerous out there, and I've been shot at, many a time."

NOT ALL BAD

It is important, he insists, not to focus on the violence of the GDs, for it gives some people the wrong impression.

Tajan throws a sign while wearing a suicide glove. He says the glove enables him to handle guns and ammunition without leaving fingerprints.

"You don't always see how important the gang is in the community," he says. "Like it's not all shooting and fighting. That's not the emphasis here. If I'd wanted a gang like that, I would have joined the Crips. I got asked, too. It was old friends of mine, kids I'd known since we were all little. And then everybody grows up; everybody gets in a gang.

"And these boys are saying, 'Hey Tajan, you want to be a Crip? You should be down with the Crips.' But I told them, 'I don't have any time for y'all.' And I meant it. Starting fights . . . man, that's just putting a target on your chest. But the GDs, like I said, they're into helping."

Noticing his visitor's dubious expression, Tajan becomes insistent.

"No, really! Listen, I want everybody to be safe. Like, there's this one woman; her name is Marlyn. She lives right across the way. Her son's bike got stolen. Well, the GDs got it back the very next day. She knows it was us that did it, too. We didn't have to do no shooting. We just control things, talk it out with the people that done it.

"Marlyn likes the GDs, man. She's a grown woman, with seven kids. She loves the GDs, 'cause she knows that the neighborhood is a lot safer with them being here than without them."

But what about the stray bullet? The cross fire from the fighting that could find Marlyn or one of her children?

Tajan shakes his head impatiently. "No, that won't happen. We control things. We don't do our battles here on our blocks. That isn't what happens. Plus, it isn't just enforcing that the GDs do; they are about making money, too. And they are about loyalty, helping each other out."

At this point in the conversation, Tajan's cousin, who calls himself A-Loc, comes into the room. He sits down in an overstuffed chair and stares at the basketball game still on television.

Tajan appeals to him: "A-Loc, tell her about how this brotherhood works."

A-Loc smiles. "Yeah, it's like everything you learn—the handshakes, the signs, everything. I learned it all from this one older dude, someone who'd been in the gang a long time before me. And he taught me how to survive, how to make my money. Then I teach it to somebody else, some younger guy later. It's a circle, a rotation. That's the beauty of it."

"Exactly," murmurs Tajan, nodding his head.

MAKING MONEY

How do people in the GDs make money? How do they teach each other to survive?

"Different ways," says A-Loc, standing up and strolling into the kitchen.

"Some sell drugs. That's one big way," says Tajan. "I mean, it's *your* hustle, you got to do whatever you got to do. Me, I'd rather get a paycheck so I don't have to deal with the police. I work at a pizza place, and that's fine for me. But other guys . . . they sell crack, some weed."

But what about the immorality of it? Doesn't the idea of selling drugs, especially to young people, seem wrong? Tajan says no.

"I don't see anything wrong with it, not really. I mean, in my mind, someone buying crack is going to smoke it whether I sell it to him or somebody else does. And the money might as well go into my pocket as that other dealer, right? But I wouldn't sell to kids. I think that's wrong. No one younger than me—no one under sixteen. I wouldn't be that desperate. But don't think they don't ask me. I mean, sometimes I'm walking around, especially by the park, and little kids come up and ask me, 'Hey, you got some weed?' I just tell them no."

QUITTING COULD BE HAZARDOUS TO YOUR HEALTH

But what if someone decided to quit the gang after he'd joined? What if he had doubts or second thoughts about some of the risks involved?

"There ain't no getting out, not really," says Tajan. "I mean, maybe there is some way, but I don't see how, myself. The idea is loyalty, and how are you going to have that if people are jumping out? To my way of thinking, leaving the gang could be hazardous to your health.

"What do I mean by that? It's simple. I know lots of guys, lots of people that are in other gangs. They know I'm a GD. Not that I'm real friendly to these guys, but I'm known. So as soon as I ain't a GD no more and the word gets out that I'm not connected, I got no GDs backing me up. I'm on my own. That means that they can go get my ass, and I'm in trouble deep.

"I don't really know why anyone would leave. I mean, even if you weren't worried about other gangs coming after you, what about your own boys?" Tajan laughs. "You could get attacked by anybody. It just depends on who comes across you. You can't be sure of anybody. There are some crazy people out there."

Would he go after a GD who left the gang?

"Naw, I don't think so, but who knows? It would depend on his reason for leaving. A *bad* reason would be that he just didn't want to be in the gang. A good reason? I don't really know. I'd have to hear a good reason. Myself, I never think about leaving, so I just couldn't tell you a good one."

LOOKING AHEAD

He can, however, foresee a time when his involvement in the day-to-day gang activity will cease. Almost everyone tapers off somewhat as they get older, he insists.

"In a way, I've kind of chilled out a little already," he says. "I am more into hanging around with my cousins, just laying low. I go to work, hang out. I am in it somewhat, but less than I was six months ago. And ten years from now? I'll be GD, for sure, but just on a different level.

"See, I know I'm going to be going to school again. I'm going to be working more, getting a better job eventually. I'm not going to be an OG, some whacker out there doing gangbanging until I'm forty. I'll still be Tajan, and I'll have that to my name. People will say, 'Hey, you guys remember Tajan?' That will be cool, being looked up to by the younger dudes. That's okay with me."

Tajan smiles when asked about his future—whether he can see himself married, with a family to help support. Although he would love to be rich, he says, he isn't sure how a family would fit into his plans.

"I have a girlfriend, yeah." He smiles. "More than one. But I don't think about that stuff. There are so many scurvy girls out there, man, girls with all sorts of diseases. Females these days think they'd all like to be players, like the boys. So they're walking around with twenty different boyfriends. Who knows what they've got? I'd rather think about making money, you know?

"I think about maybe getting into real estate, investing in some house and selling it for a big profit. I've heard there are millions to be made in real estate if you do it right. If I had money now, I think I'd buy my mom a new house or something. Then I'd buy a car, or maybe two of them, and move somewhere else. Probably California. I know I wouldn't be here, in this neighborhood. Maybe I'd go to some high school and get on some team somewhere, get back into that for a while."

So Many Problems

Reality is far different, however, and Tajan doesn't dwell long on daydreams. He is sixteen, half African American and half white, and a Gangster Disciple. It bothers him, he says, that those three characteristics can be taken so negatively by other people who don't know him at all.

"I know all about stereotypes," he says. "I know what white people think about black people. It's the same with gangs. People think we're all bad, like we're not worth anything because we're affiliated. But the way I think is that you can't judge something you don't know anything about. What I say is just talk to a person, listen to what that person has to say. Like we're doing here, right?

"See, if you see me on the street, maybe you're thinking, 'Uh-oh, I better get in and lock my door. This dude looks like trouble—bandanna, baggy pants, half black.' So that's what you see and what you're thinking. But me? Maybe I'm thinking, 'Hey, I wonder if she wants to sell that car?'

"You know? We're on different levels. So I talk to someone, and they act all nervous, like they think I'm going to take a gun out and shoot them or something. And that makes me mad, that they're acting nervous, acting like I'm bad. And that makes me feel real bad inside."

Tajan smiles. "It's just getting around all that outside stuff that's hard. I'm smart enough to understand that some of this gang stuff scares people. Just like when I went for my job interview at the pizza place, I had to lose the bandanna, lose the baggy pants. I got to work my way in; I know that.

"But even without the baggy pants or the bandanna, the things I think about . . . those things aren't going to change. I don't want to be scaring nobody, because when people are scared they do stupid things. But what I think and how I feel about stuff inside my head, that's my own business. And inside my head, I'm a GD."

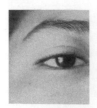

Edwin

"THERE ARE A LOT OF LITTLE
KIDS WHO SEE OLDER GUYS
DOING STUFF, AND IT LOOKS
COOL TO THEM. SO THEY START
LEARNING THE SIGNS, DOING ALL
THE GANG STUFF. BUT YOU
KNOW, IT'S REALLY STUPID. WE
TELL THE LITTLE KIDS THAT."

Edwin is tall and good-looking, with the long legs that are the sign of a growing sixteen-year-old boy. His legs, at the present, are up on a coffee table in his living room, as he sits on a sofa.

He is, he explains, "sort of in a gang"—the Latin Kings. Although he has not yet gone through the initiation, the jumping in, as it is called, he says he is as much a part of the gang as his friends who already have been jumped in. He will talk about the gang, but he is nervous. Edwin does not want his picture taken, he says, because he is not sure what some of the other gang members would feel about him telling things to an outsider.

"Maybe in a couple more years I would feel different," he says, shrugging. "But right now I'm not in a good position to be making decisions like that. It's not like I know lots of secrets or anything. But I'd rather not have anybody know it was me you got this information about the gang from, okay?"

Edwin is Latino; he came to the United States from El Salvador when he was seven years old. It was important to his mother that they flee their homeland because of the civil war there.

"I remember it, sure," he says with enthusiasm. "I know about the war there, about the fighting. My mom was the one who came to the United States first. She met some people—Nick and Jesse. They are Americans, and they made friends with my mother. They helped her get some papers or something. See, she'd had to sneak across the border because she was illegal.

"My sister—she's three years older than me—was living with my aunt back in El Salvador while my mother was away. I was living with my grandma. Anyway, when it was time for us to come across—my sister and me—we had papers. We didn't have to sneak. My sister came first, and then [my mother] sent for me."

Edwin says that although there was a war going on in his country, it wasn't until he came to the United States that he understood why.

"I didn't understand lots of things," he says. "It wasn't until last year, when I was visiting my cousins in California, that they told me about what was going on in my country. I heard about the government, how they are doing all kinds of bad stuff to the people.

"Man, I didn't even know about that when it was happening. I mean, I can remember soldiers coming into our village and busting into our house. They'd line everybody up against the wall like they were going to shoot us. But they didn't. They just scared us so that we'd let them stay there to sleep or rest for a while.

"The government was really strict and didn't care about the people. So the people came up with their own army, the guerrillas. So the guerrillas, like my cousins and my uncles, were busy fighting. And the government was searching everywhere for the guerillas so they could kill them. And if they couldn't find the guerrillas, they'd find their families and their houses and destroy them. Like, they'd burn houses—whole villages of people. And they'd torture the mothers and fathers of the guerrillas and kill their animals."

"A Scary Place"

Edwin says he was amazed when his relatives filled him in on what had been going on in El Salvador.

"It's a scary place," he says, shaking his head. "I think about that, about how I was there when it was going on, and I kind of get scared all over again. Scared in reverse, like. I mean, those government dudes are bad. If you do anything wrong, they kill you. No trial, nothing.

"I mean, even if you don't do bad stuff, they kill you. Lots of people die over there for no reason, man. One of my uncles . . .

they took him, just took him. He never came back. Probably got killed, tortured. Sometimes they find those guys later, with parts of their body cut off or burned or whatever. Like ears, fingers—stuff you don't even want to think about. And lots of those people who disappeared, they never get buried, never have a funeral for their family, nothing. Just lying in a ditch somewhere, tortured to death, man. I think what my uncle had done was talk back or something once when they broke into his house.

"I hear about it from my relatives here," he explains. "My one aunt sometimes tells my mother what she hears from back in El Salvador. It gradually gets around to me, I guess. It's not something I think about all the time, but once in a while, I kind of imagine what it would be like if I was still living there. Or I think about how my little cousins are holding up."

BIGGER AND MEANER

Edwin says that besides squads of guerrilla fighters in El Salvador, there are also gangs.

"That maybe surprises people," he says. "People in the United States think gangs are just a problem here, or whatever. Or they think it's a city deal, but it's not. I won't say the gangs are the same as here, because they're not. They're worse.

"They aren't the same as the guerrillas, no. See, when I was little, there weren't too many gangs there. But now they have formed gangs, just like over here. Like, where we lived in El Salvador, there were mostly forests and stuff and rivers and big old passageways that lead up to the volcanos; that's like the areas of different gangs. Yeah, like the turf [territory], or whatever they call it.

"They are really deadly over there, too. I mean it," Edwin says emphatically. "I mean, if there was a gang war over there, it would be like armies fighting over here. They don't wear colors, like here. No rags [bandannas] or nothing, no jerseys. At least, not that I know about. They want to fit in, see. They don't want no one to know what they're doing.

"And they are really armed. You know, around here, a gang fights with maybe little nines [nine-millimeter guns], while there it is, like, machine guns, grenades, M16s, everything. It's like an arsenal, man. And they got strange names, like the Mau Mau. That's the gang my cousins belong to.

"They do drug dealing, too, just like over here. Actually, they do a lot more, since they grow so much marijuana over there, you know. They sell it and send it over here to make money. I don't know the details, you know, because I wasn't into that then. I was too little. But I know those gangs are into it big.

"See, the gangs help out the guerrillas over there. The guerrillas get lots of their money for guns and stuff from the gangs. That's why there's that tie-in between the gangs and the guerrillas. It's like the guerrillas kind of sponsor the gangs, help protect them."

Edwin says that most gangs in the United States are made up of teenagers but that there are a lot of older people in El Salvadoran gangs.

"Whoever wants to can join," he says. "Each gang is managed by a guerrilla leader, like I said. They are connected. And one important thing is that the guerrillas try to keep the peace over there, too. See, the government wants to destroy the gangs, since they are helping the guerrillas. They even got a government death squad over there called the Black Shadow. They go around killing guys they think are gang members.

Edwin says the gangs in his homeland of El Salvador are bigger and more dangerous than the gangs in the United States. "If there was a gang war over there, it would be like armies fighting over here."

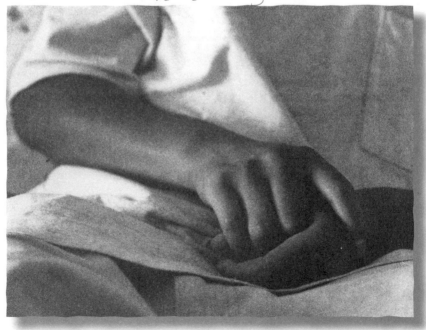

"So the gangs keep a low profile—way different from here. I mean, they're bigger, they're meaner, but they're quieter, too. They do too much fighting, and the Black Shadow comes in, see? They got to be careful, since it affects the civil war over there."

SHE THREW ME OUT

Edwin's own affiliation with American gangs came later, after he had been in the United States a number of years. But even before then, he found himself getting into trouble in his new home.

"My mom got a job right away when we got here," he says. "Those people she'd made friends with hired her to be a kind of live-in housekeeper and baby-sitter. So me and my sister and my mom lived with their family.

"It wasn't a bad setup, I guess. I mean, it was a nice old house, not too far from the lake. But I kind of got into some fights with their kids, and after a while, we moved out of there. We came here, to this apartment building. She still works for them, but the kids are old enough not to need a full-time baby-sitter anyway. She cleans, does stuff like that. They like her. She's like one of the family, I guess."

But moving to the apartment only resulted in more problems within his family, he says. Several months ago his mother threw him out of the house because of what she claimed was "violent, threatening behavior" toward her.

"I think things are changing for me, things between my mom and me," he says. "Back before she threw me out, we had been arguing a lot. I just didn't get along with her, I guess. I don't know . . . she'd get mad at me for lots of things I did. Little stuff sometimes, like not doing my jobs, talking back to her, things about school.

"I wasn't in trouble too much in school back then. I fought sometimes, but that's about it. You want an example of what me and my mom would get into a fight about? Well, like if I stayed out too late, or I was hanging out too much at my girlfriend's house or with my friends.

"What would happen is that we would physically fight a lot," he explains. "She'd push me, because she didn't like the tone of my voice. And so I'd push her back. Stuff like that. I didn't hit her, not really. I mean, if she hit me, I'd wrestle her to keep her from hitting me again. Maybe to her it seemed like I was hitting, but it was, like, self-defense. I couldn't handle her grabbing me, pushing me. And because I couldn't handle it, she told me I had to leave. She didn't think it was right for me to stay there, acting the way I was acting, I guess."

Edwin's aunt in California agreed to let him spend some time there, but Edwin says that didn't work out well.

"My aunt is strict, like my mom," he says. "So I got in trouble there, too. I stayed out late, did things she didn't like. It was just like a replay of here, only different weather. So after about eight months, they sent me back home."

TAKING HIS TIME

Edwin says that one of the problems he had while staying with his aunt in California was his involvment with a gang there, although he was never officially a member.

"It was a gang called the Mexican Mafia, and they were really bad," he says. "I didn't do too much with them. I went on a drive-by one time and got arrested. See, I was going to get paid two hundred dollars to beat somebody up at the high school. But I didn't end up doing it, because somebody called the police. Some security guy called, I think.

"What happened was, we saw the kid I was supposed to beat up, and one of the guys I was with grabbed him. They started wrestling, and I was just ready to start beating on him when the security guy yelled at us. The cops came screaming up, and we got caught. We got arrested then, but they didn't have any priors [prior arrest information] on me, so they let me go. My friend, the one who grabbed the guy, he went to jail for a minute or two, but he ended up getting out on thirty-six hundred dollars' bail."

Since coming home, Edwin says, he has made some close friends who are in the Latin Kings gang, and he is very close to joining them.

"I've done lots of stuff with them," he says, "but I'm not officially in; I haven't been jumped in. Almost all the guys I know in the gang are old friends from grade school. One guy, Jose, I'm especially good friends with. We'd always hung out before, but I don't know, we sort of went different ways for a while. Jose went off to Mexico for a while, and I left for California for eight months.

"Anyway, I came back and saw him again and met lots of these other Hispanic kids I hadn't seen for a while. They were asking

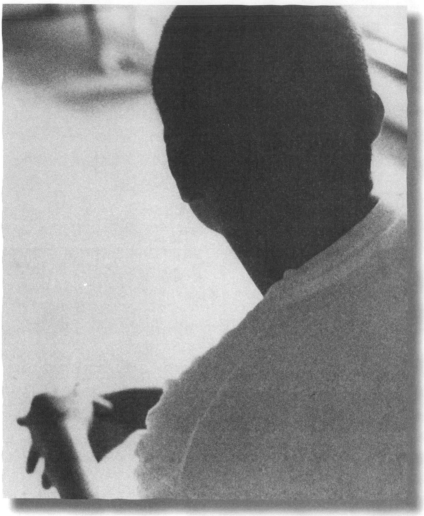

Despite his mother's efforts to protect him, Edwin became involved with a gang after he moved to California.

me to get in, but I was, like, 'Not now. Kick it! I'll just be hanging around with you guys.' I didn't want to join right away."

Asked why he was hesitant, Edwin smiles and shrugs.

"I don't know. You just can't be getting in right away. You got to take your time, make sure this is what you want to do, before you join. I met a lot of them, a lot of the Kings, and they're all right. But I'm just being cautious, you know? They're nice guys; they don't go around looking for trouble all the time. But if trouble comes, they'll go at it. They know what they're doing."

TROUBLE WITH THE BOGUS BOYS

Edwin says that this summer has been an especially difficult time for the Latin Kings. Several of their leaders have been arrested on drug charges, while just a week ago some of them had guns taken away.

"They were in a war with a new gang called the Bogus Boys," he explains. "They're a black gang and really bad. You don't know what they're going to do. They are like a bunch of Vice Lords, Crips, and GDs put together. There were drive-bys every night—lots of action between the Kings and the Bogus Boys. A busy time and a lot of shooting.

"I was in California for a visit when it all was happening, but my friends were telling me about it. They were waiting, figuring the Bogus Boys were going to show up at this one location. But who shows up is the police. And the Kings had all their weapons, all of them. So the cops just came and arrested them all, took all their guns. Sure, the Bogus Boys must have snitched to the cops. That's what happened."

What has become of the war between the gangs?

"Oh, the Bogus Boys are around, yeah," he says. "More now than before. They're into lots of stuff around this neighborhood, and like I said, they're crazy. You can't predict what they're going to do next. See, when a gang is new, they're all about trying to establish their reputation. They want to be hard, they want to be known. That means if you're in another gang, you better watch out. Around here, the reputation of a gang or a set can change overnight. They're a growing gang, too, for being so new. They had only about 30 guys last year, but now they got about 110. That's scary."

COLORS, BRAND NAMES, AND SHOELACES

Edwin says that it is easy to spot Latin Kings, for like most other gangs in town, they have an established set of colors their members wear.

"We got gold and black," he says. "We wear lots of black, especially black shirts. Lots of Kings wear Dickies; they're like work pants, kind of khaki. We wear them baggy, too.

"For shirts, they wear this one style called Ben Davis. It's just a brand from California. Usually we get them in any color; it doesn't have to be gold or black. Just not blue, though—that's GDs and

Crips. We stay away from lots of shirts and jerseys because they are already claimed by other gangs. Like Crips will wear a lot of North Carolina jerseys, that light blue. We don't wear Notre Dame either; that's GDs. Myself, I wear Dickies and different shirts—usually plain black shirts, I guess. I don't have any Ben Davis stuff yet, but I might get that stuff sometime soon.

"Shoes are a way you can sometimes tell a King, too. Like, mostly we wear Nike, with a white lace hooked over the top, see?" He lifts up his shoe to demonstrate. "Sometimes you can tell a King because of that, but not all the time. But one time I was in a lockup facility downtown—it was for violating curfew—and I met a guy in there. He told me he knew I was a King. I asked him how, and he told me it was because of that top lace."

How are these things decided—who wears what color, how shoes are laced? Edwin doesn't know, but he assumes it's the OGs, the original gangsters, who have been around the longest.

"I'm not in on it, anyway," he says, smiling. "They don't ask me. But there are leaders of the Kings. They're from Chicago. I'm sure they tell people what's going on, what kinds of things to do. And what the OGs are wearing, I'm sure the others wear, too. I don't know *where* these decisions are made, either. But I do know that a lot of the big decisions are made at their meetings."

AT THE MEETING

Edwin says that gang meetings are held on a regular basis. Although as a nonmember he probably shouldn't have gone, he did accompany his friend Jose to a meeting.

"Me and Jose took a bus over to this place where the Kings usually are kicking it. They call it *la vicinda*. I guess that just means, like, 'the neighborhood'—something like that. It's just an area over west, on the corner of Twenty-eighth and Chapel. Anyway, Jose said I could go even though it was supposed to be just gang members.

"There were about twenty or twenty-five people there. I guess they just spread the word a few days before, and people showed up. I was curious about what it would be like. So when everybody was there, they are, like, doing their handshakes, all the Kings. And anyway, there's a leader who's older—maybe in his thirties, I guess. He starts it out, collects five bucks from everyone. There's a treasurer who holds the money.

"I asked Jose what the money is for. He says it's for bail or for buying weapons if there's a war. Or other things, too, like one of the Kings had got shot in the leg, so we're using the money to help him out, get him a place to stay. See, he's had problems with his parents, so we're all the family he has right now, the only ones he can depend on until he's back on his feet.

"Anyway, at that meeting it was pretty calm, considering one of our guys had gotten shot. But see, we want revenge, but the Crip that did it is in jail already. So we're waiting for the right time to get him. Not yet, though, 'cause like I said, our leaders are in jail themselves right now."

"We Got Plenty of Backup"

Edwin estimates that there are about thirty active Latin Kings in the area but stresses that there are several branches, or sets, in addition to those.

"There's the West Side Kings, the Riverside Kings, and a new one called the UCK—the Unknown City Kings," he says. "They just started up, so they're small. But they're pretty ruthless, I guess. And if we ever get into a situation where we need help, all we gotta do is call Chicago and we got plenty of backup."

Most of the Kings show up at the meetings, he says, because they are usually anxious to know what is going on, especially new developments in wars with other gangs.

"And if they need another reason to get there, and that isn't enough," he says, "then they should worry about getting a violation. That's, like, a beating for not showing up at a meeting. Like, if it was Jose that didn't show, whenever two people from the Kings see him next, they beat him up for thirty seconds. And he just has to take it. They can't do no mouth or nose shots, though—nothing on the face."

"They're Shaking 'Cause They're So Nervous"

How many violations are Kings allowed? Edwin laughs.

"You mean, is it like speeding tickets they keep count of? No, there ain't no limit. It's not like you're going to get kicked out of the gang. I guess if you can stand getting beat up, you can keep getting them. Most people don't get many, though. They don't want to. They're usually conscious afterwards, but they're shaking 'cause they're so nervous."

By his own admission, a good deal of the time in a gang is spent kicking it, or hanging out, with fellow gang members, with no particular aim in mind.

"They hang out a lot at *la vicinda*," he says. "Some of the guys have jobs, but mostly in the afternoon they're over there. It's just a little place, an apartment building on the corner where most of them live, you know?"

Is it dangerous for someone other than a King to walk by *la vicinda*?

It depends, Edwin says.

"Like, you could go through there, no problem. You don't look like you are claiming anything. I mean, just a person, there's no big risk. It just depends, though. I mean, it has to do with how you are dressed, how you are walking. If you are dressed normally, I guess we wouldn't do anything. But if the person's got on a blue shirt, something would happen, yeah. Red? Probably nothing, because we're cool with the Bloods."

"You Gotta Pay Attention"

"You gotta know signs if you're in a gang like the Kings. Everybody knows everyone's signs. Like if they throw it at us, we have to know what it means. You just can't throw it around. Some people are really crazy; they shoot you over doing something wrong. You might be doing it wrong—throwing their sign [upside] down, disrespecting it without meaning to—if you didn't know the sign. You gotta pay attention.

"With the Kings, our sign is the crown. We may not shoot someone for disrespecting the crown, but we won't let it go by, either. I mean, it's important. That's a thing we all got. Like one time, me and my friends Miguel, Jose, and Sleepy were walking around, and we saw some GD who looked at us and put down the crown—just did it upside down. We beat him up for that, no problem.

"The next day some GDs come walking through *la vicinda* with a pole and everything, ready to retaliate for that. But there were cops around, so nothing happened. Anyway, later on this one GD comes up to me, and he says, 'How come you guys jumped that GD the other day?' He called me a buster. That's, like, a guy who goes around beating people up all the time; it's an insult. But we told him, 'Man, he was putting down the crown. We threw that start up, and he put it down. We won't take that. You can't put down the crown.'"

MIGUEL

The worst thing that has happened in his association with the Latin Kings, he says, is the death of his good friend Miguel. It is something he cannot talk about without tears.

"I wasn't there when Miguel got shot, but I came up just a few minutes later," he says softly. "I saw him lying there dead. I don't even know why they shot him, really. This was about three weeks ago. He was usually real calm, never started stuff. He didn't get into trouble claiming stuff around other gangs. He got along with people, usually.

"Miguel and another friend of mine were walking back to his house, and they decided to go get something to eat, I guess. Anyway, a guy came up to them at an intersection real close to *la vicinda* and said, 'L-K-K.' That means, Latin King Killer. And then they shot Miguel in the head.

"I was at *la vicinda* with some other people, and we heard the

"You gotta know signs if you're in a gang like the Kings," says Edwin. If you throw a sign wrong, he says, you run the risk of getting shot.

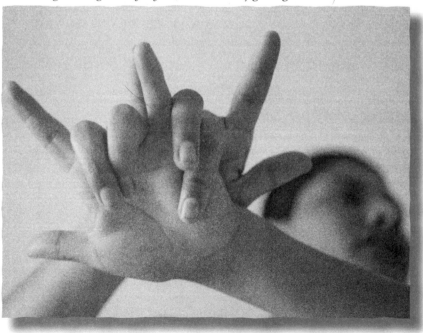

shots. We ran over there and saw my other friend, the one who was with Miguel when it happened. And I looked and I saw Miguel just lying there between two parked cars.

"I asked my friend what happened. Over and over I kept saying, 'How did he get shot? What happened to him?' But he didn't know. My friend just said that as soon as the guy shot Miguel, my other friend went and hid under a car so they didn't go after him, too. Just Miguel."

"IT JUST SEEMED LIKE MAYBE IT WAS ALL A MISTAKE"

Edwin says that although he tries to forget seeing Miguel that night, the image keeps haunting him.

"There was so much blood," he says. "He got shot five times in the back besides getting it in the head. I remember looking at him, seeing him lying there, but not believing it was real. What I was seeing seemed like something that should be in somebody's else's life, not mine. You know?

"We just stood there in the street, I remember that. The police got there pretty fast. They were nice. It seemed like they weren't saying too much. I kept saying, 'Will he be okay?' even though I knew Miguel was dead. I don't know why I asked that. It just seemed like maybe it was all a mistake and he was breathing after all. Just the way he looked made it seem like he might be alive. If you could forget that there was all that blood, you couldn't really see his wounds. He was lying on his front, but his head was turned to the side. I don't know . . . maybe it's just because I wanted him not to be dead that he seemed like he wasn't."

The police caught the person who shot Miguel, Edwin says, although there was still no clear explanation of why the boy had shot Miguel.

"The guy was a Crip," he says in a flat voice. "He got charged with first-degree murder. He'll be in there for life. Who cares about him? I don't. The other guy, the one who had been driving the car, he got twenty years, I guess.

"Miguel went to a school where there were a lot of Crips. It was like an alternative school for kids with problems. Mostly all the Crips I talked to said the same thing, that Miguel was pretty calm. He didn't have trouble getting along. It seems so mysterious to me, how he could be alive one second, and the next second he was in the street with all those policemen standing over him. Like, where did the part that was alive go? I don't know. I keep thinking about that and it scares me. I just miss Miguel."

Miguel's funeral was a very sad affair, he says, because of how devastated Miguel's family was.

"I just remember Miguel was all laid out, black pants and a white shirt," he says. "His dad knew about his being a King. He understood, I think, because they are from Chicago, and there are lots of Kings there, lots of gangs. They came here to get away from the gangs, but Miguel found it here. His dad had to know that there were gangs here, too. I guess they're everywhere. The risk is always there. It's just the life he had, you know?"

ALWAYS A RISK

Edwin has been attacked by other gangs, too. Although none of the instances has resulted in serious injury, he says that he is more watchful than ever since Miguel's death.

"I got jumped not too far from here by eight Crips," he says. "Yeah, the Crips don't get along with Kings at all. I had been at the Y, and some kids there started some trouble. They asked me what I was claiming and everything, and I told them no, that I'm not in any gang. I told them I didn't want no trouble. But the one guy hit me in the face. Then I was going to hit him back, but another guy steps out and grabs my hand. All of a sudden there were six more. I got away running and just kept going. I mean, I have no problem with running away.

"Sometimes it seems like there is going to be real trouble, you know, but for some reason it doesn't happen. Like, the other day I was walking to my friend's house, and I went into a store. There were ten Crips there, just hanging out. I saw this one girl I knew. She lives near *la vicinda*. I started talking to her, when all of a sudden I had this feeling like the Crips were coming up on me to grab me.

"Three of them walked behind the store, two went inside, and more came right over by me. It seemed like they were planning something. The ones by me were staring at me, really looking me over. I didn't say nothing because I was alone. I'd have fought them if they came at me, but I knew I'd lose, you know?

"So I was standing there, holding my bag, ready to throw it at them if they started something. But they didn't do anything. They

Since his friend Miguel was killed by gang members, Edwin says he is more watchful. "You just gotta watch your back."

just asked that girl if she knew me, if I was her boyfriend or whatever. And one guy calls me *esse* which is what a lot of us call 'homeboy'—just a Spanish way of saying it, you know? Lots of black gang guys picked it up; they use it like, 'What's up, *esse*?' That's the style from California; lots of guys imitate that. So anyway, that ended up being no problem. But you just never know."

"YOU JUST GOTTA WATCH YOUR BACK"

"And after what happened to Miguel, I know I'm more nervous than usual," he admits. "You just gotta watch your back. Like, one time I was on my way to work, and I ran into a whole bunch of Bogus Boys and GDs. There were about seven Bogus Boys, and a GD in the middle. All of a sudden, they were, like, saying, 'Hey, he's a King, get him!' I was scared, but that GD says, 'Naw, man, I know him; I'm cool with him.' They think I'm a King, since I hang out with Kings. But that was close. That's another fight I would have lost, for sure."

Does he carry a weapon for situations like these?

"I used to have to cross over a place where all the GDs hang out

46

when I worked at the park," he says. "I'd carry a knife or two with me then. But I don't do that anymore. See, I decided I don't want no job where I have to walk through that park. I was a staff person, answering phones and stuff, but it wasn't worth it. You might get off at 9:00 and they would be waiting for you to pass by, kill you right on the spot. Naw, I don't want to be in situations like these, where you can't watch your back. Too dangerous. I'd rather wait and find another job somewhere safe."

"NEVER KILL A LITTLE KID"

There are a lot of stereotypes people have about kids in gangs, Edwin says. He wishes that people would get to know more kids so that they would understand that gangs are not a way for kids to terrorize people.

"It's not like that," he insists. "If you're minding your own business and everything, we won't bother you. It's just that we know that there are a lot of people out to get us. Like over near *la vicinda* there are a lot of Bogus Boys, Crips, GDs—lots of black people who hate the Kings. I mean, most everybody over there is in a gang of some sort or another.

"See, the black gangs are coming into that area, but that area has been Hispanic for a long time. So there's trouble. We gotta protect our neighborhood, man. But you understand that everything that happens happens for a reason. I mean, I don't know about Miguel, but there's probably a reason I don't know yet for that happening. Even if it's a bad reason or a mistake or something. Even if it's just being in the wrong place at the wrong time."

But what about innocent people being killed in cross fire? What about the instances of children playing on their own porches getting hit by stray bullets from rival gangs? Why do we hear so often about gangs firing indiscriminately at a crowd of people and killing people who have nothing to do with their rivalry with another gang?

Edwin nods. "I know what you mean. That's bad, when kids get hurt. I don't know how they plan things here, but in California, when I used to hang around with the Mexican Mafia, they teach you to avoid kids. Like, the way they teach you is, never kill a little kid. Like, if you're going for someone in the house, you kill every adult that's there, but you never touch a kid. Or you can risk getting killed yourself.

"But," he says, "you gotta know that there are kids in gangs, even young kids. There's a King in town here who is only eleven. He's no wanna-be, either. He's a real King, in fifth grade up at Hills [Elementary School]. So if you're in a gang war, just 'cause a kid gets shot at doesn't necessarily mean it's some innocent victim. There's lots of younger guys in gangs.

"Wanna-bes. Yeah, that's kind of a problem. There are a lot of little kids who see older guys doing stuff, and it looks cool to them. So they start learning the signs, doing all the gang stuff. But you know, it's really stupid. We tell the little kids that. When they pretend they're Kings, they're taking all the risks, but they're getting none of the advantages.

"Like if they throw a sign up or they disrespect some other gang's sign, they take the consequences. They usually get no real help from the Kings, either, unless we happen to be there at the time something happens. They're on their own. We tell the kids, Don't throw stuff up if you ain't in the gang, but they don't listen. I know at *la vicinda* most of their moms make them stay inside the building. They don't even get to come outside too much on their own. It's not safe out there, really. Even a real little kid could get in serious trouble if he makes the wrong move and a Bogus Boy or Crip or something sees him."

DANGER AT *LA VICINDA*

Edwin says he is glad that so many of the mothers around *la vicinda* are protective of their children, for it gets dangerous there. Even for older, well-armed gang members, he says, the place is risky.

"It's no wonder that lots of the kids around there have weapons," he says with a shrug. "I guess it's mostly nine millimeters, and they're not cheap. I guess they're around five hundred dollars each out on the street. I mean, you can get them in stores, but they're lots more expensive, plus you can get traced. Lots of guys carry the nine mils pretty much all the time around *la vicinda* just because of the shooting that happens there a lot.

"I mean, yesterday, the Kings had a big gun war over there with this new gang called the Bishops. The Bishops came rolling around here fast, like it was going to be a drive-by. You know how those cars go real fast around and around? I wasn't at *la vicinda* when it happened because I was at my girlfriend's house, but I heard all about it.

48

"Anyway, they slowed down for a second and talked to one of the Kings, and the King pulled out a gun and started shooting. The Bishop car kept rolling around so fast they were going to kill the Kings, it seemed like. Then at the same time another group of Kings started shooting, too, and then more Bishops were firing. It ended up nobody got killed, but it's hard to see how. Like I said before, *la vicinda* is no place just to be hanging around, especially if you aren't looking for trouble."

NOT EVERYTHING IS ABOUT GANGS

Although Edwin is involved with many of the Latin Kings, and much of his activity centers around them, there are other things in his life.

"I've got a girlfriend that I'm pretty serious about," he says shyly. "Her name is Sofia, and she lives kind of near *la vicinda*. I go over there a lot to see her. No, she's not in the gang. I mean, there *are* some Latin Queens [female members of the Latin Kings], but not too many around here. She does have connections in the gang, though.

"See, her uncle is one of the Kings leaders. Sofia knows I'm associated with the Kings; she knows I'm seriously thinking about getting jumped in. She says that she worries about me but that she knows I'll do what I need to. She tells me to watch out. That's all she can do. With her uncle and everything, she knows better than lots of people how bad it can get.

"Last year she would hang around with some of the King boys a lot outside *la vicinda*. One time though, this Bogus Boy leader shot at them with a Mac-10. That guy lives in the next building over. I don't know why he did it. Sofia never found out, either. She didn't get hurt, but she was really scared afterwards, so she stopped hanging around over there. Just mostly me, that's who she's with."

Edwin says that he has a lot on his mind now, and much of it centers around his stormy relationship with his mother.

"I think she just doesn't understand how it is, growing up here. She had trouble with my sister, too, when my sister was my age. But now my sister is nineteen, and they are getting along better. I hope that happens with me, too.

"I want to get along with my mom. I hate fighting with her all the time. Ever since I got back from California, we've had some big fights. Right now it's worse. I can feel it. Today she's not mad at me, but two days ago she was. It was about school then, because

A caricature of Edwin hangs above a mirror in his bedroom. Edwin wishes his home life would improve, especially his relationship with his mother: "She thinks I don't care, but I do."

I was doing bad. I missed a lot of days, 'cause I skip a lot. I go over to see Sofia; she skips, too. But I'm doing bad right now in three of my classes, so my mom is still going to be mad.

"If I could get my wish, I'd wish we could get along for a while. I hope there's not going to be a thing like what happened last year, when she got so mad she threw me out. I felt bad all the time last year, it seems like. She doesn't know me, I don't think. She doesn't know how mad I get inside, or how sad I feel sometimes. She thinks I don't care, but I do."

Kim

"FOR SOME PEOPLE WHO DON'T
HAVE THE FAMILY THEY NEED,
THEIR GANG IS ALL THEY KNOW,
ALL THEY HAVE. IT'S SOMETHING
JUST FOR YOU, SOMETHING YOU
HAVE FOR YOUR OWN."

"I got in a fight with this one girl last night. I knew I was getting my picture taken today, and I didn't want her messing with my face. She would have, too. I had to hurt her, but it doesn't really bother me. The fights . . . they happen less often now, anyway."

The toughness of the words do not match the soft voice and the petite form of the young woman talking. She is small boned, with curly dark hair, and has a model's good looks. Her name, she says, is Kim, and she is a Vice Lord. The latter she says with pride and adds that although she is twenty years old now and the mother of a small child, she is no less a Vice Lord in her heart than she was back when she was a young teen.

"I mean, you never really stop, right?" she says with a slight smile. "I stopped being real active when I got pregnant. But I'm still affiliated with them; I still hang out with them. I don't think I could ever *not* be a Vice Lord, you know what I mean? I'm just not into it right now the same as I was back a few years. It doesn't mean that I won't be that same way again, though."

"A BAD LITTLE KID"

No one should be surprised that a young woman can be a member of the Vice Lords, according to Kim. There are plenty of girls out there who are just as tough as the boys.

"Sure there's girl Vice Lords," she says. "I'm sure there are girls in every gang. There should be; it isn't just boys who can fight. I've always been tough—always. I should have known that I would be in some gang eventually. Even at a real early age, you know?

"I was a bad little kid. I was bad tempered, bratty, always had to have my own way. I still remember beating up my younger sister all the time. I wouldn't listen to nobody. I guess it's because I needed to be the one who got her way. I hated people telling me what to do or what not to do. My mom was afraid of me sometimes, I think. I was a little more scared of my dad. He was a semi driver, so he was gone a lot. My mom worked, too—she has a housecleaning business—but she was always home in the evenings. But my dad had a louder voice, and I knew I couldn't pull quite as much on him as I did on my mom."

School, Kim says, was more of the same.

"I hated it, just hated it," she says, frowning. "They had to physically put me on the bus in the mornings. I didn't like the teacher in kindergarten, even, telling me to do things different, helping me with my printing, or whatever. I didn't like school, and I wasn't good at it, either. Maybe I could have been, I don't know. But I didn't want to do whatever the teachers wanted."

"I THREW THE BOOK AT HER"

In grade school, Kim says, she was contrary and sassy. But by the time she got to junior high and high school, she was uncontrollable.

"I acted out a lot in junior high," she admits. "I got snotty to the teachers a lot. And in high school I started getting belligerent. I cussed out the teachers a lot. There was this one woman who was just stupid—just stupid—and racist, I think, too. She made me sit in the front row all the time in her class. And this one time she told me to do something—it was to open my book to some page or other—and I didn't do it.

"So then she gets all mad. She says, 'Kim, what's the matter with you? I said open your book, right now!' I said to her, 'What did you say?' And she says, 'Are you stupid, or what? I said open your book like I told you, like I told everyone else.'

"So I just cussed at her, told her what I thought of her calling me stupid, and I threw the book at her. Right at her head. I got sent to the office and got in more trouble there."

Kim sighs. A bored look is on her face. "I couldn't care less, you know? I mean, she didn't respect me, so she didn't deserve any from me is the way I look at it."

LEARNING ABOUT GANGS

Kim's interest in gangs started with her cousins, she says. They lived on the west side of the city.

Kim contends that there are many girls who are just as tough as boys. "I'm sure there are girls in every gang. There should be; it isn't just boys who can fight."

"See, I'd go stay there sometimes during the day when my mom was at work, like on the weekends or during the summer. I stayed with my grandma sometimes, too. I really liked it at my cousins'. They were so much fun to be around. They are part Native American, part Mexican, and they're all Vice Lords.

"My cousins were all girls, except one. And even when I was really young, I knew about their being in a gang, because their dads were, too. They just grew up around it. All of the older cousins would be there, in the house, and I'd watch them throwing their signs around and see them wearing their colors. I guess I'd have had to be pretty dumb not to figure it out after a while."

Were her uncles still active in the Vice Lords? She shakes her head.

"No, they were just in it, you know? Not into the whole thing with fighting and stuff. But they were proud to be Vice Lords. They'd talk to us sometimes, especially when we got to the age where we were wanting to be in the gang too. They'd tell stories about the gang when they were young.

"They'd give us advice, too, about what to do, what not to do. Like they said don't get a bad name fighting all the time; then you get known as a buster. And don't be real obvious about what we claim, about what signs we throw up. In other words, don't go looking for trouble all the time. They said we'd live longer that way. Lay low, they said, keep quiet. See, they were real serious about that, because one of the older cousins had been killed when I was really little. He was real loud about claiming his gang and got killed in a drive-by."

JUMPING IN

Although her cousins were initiated into the gang before she was, Kim says that she felt that she was a Vice Lord long before she was jumped in.

"I finally decided to go ahead with it at a Vice Lords picnic," she remembers. "I was already dressing in the colors. We'd wear red all the time, with these khaki pants called Dickies. Red rags around our heads, too. I was doing things with my cousins all the time. We'd be hanging together almost every weekend, and all summer. So what was the difference, I figured."

What are Vice Lords picnics like? Do they all dress in red, and do they fight with other picnickers in the park? Kim smiles.

"I guess in a way it sounds kind of odd, like a church picnic or a bunch of Shriners, or whatever those old guys are called. But no, they don't get into any fighting. Yeah, they wear red, lots of red. But they bring their kids, grill hamburgers, do the same things everyone else does at a picnic, I guess. I'm sure some of them have guns, yeah. I don't think all of them do, but some."

She pauses a moment to get her bearings.

"So at the picnic, one of the leaders just asked if there was anyone who was being jumped in that night. Everybody looked at me, like, 'Are you, or aren't you?' I was kind of pressured, yeah. I mean, the only way I could have easily stayed out of the Vice Lords was to stay home, stay out of the west side. But I didn't want to do that. I liked being with my cousins. They were family. I felt closer to them than I did my parents and sisters!"

Did she have to read something about the gang before she was jumped in? Did she know what she was getting into?

"The GDs, they make you read all that junk about Larry Hoover," she says, nodding. "No, the Vice Lords don't get into that. They figure you are joining because you got a reason to join. I knew it was about respecting your neighborhood, being loyal to other people in the gang. Stick together, help each other out. Not real complicated.

"But I had a choice about how to get in. As a girl, I could choose having sex with people in the gang—that's called rolling your way in—or fighting my way in. I chose fighting. I wasn't about to do that other thing! I figured, when you come right down to it, with all the diseases and everything, I'd be a lot safer fighting against five gang members."

She fought for five minutes against five Vice Lords girls, and it wasn't easy at all.

"Hey, most of those five were cousins," she says with a smile. "And they weren't going easy at all on me. I mean, maybe *they* thought they were being kind, but it hurt a lot. I got hit hard, a couple of times in the back of my head. That hurt for a long time afterwards. And they're not allowed to hit you in the face during the jumping in—no breaking noses or whatever."

"WE WERE HAVING SOME REALLY GOOD TIMES"

Kim remembers her early years in the gang with fondness. "I was hanging with my cousins all the time," she says, "and we were

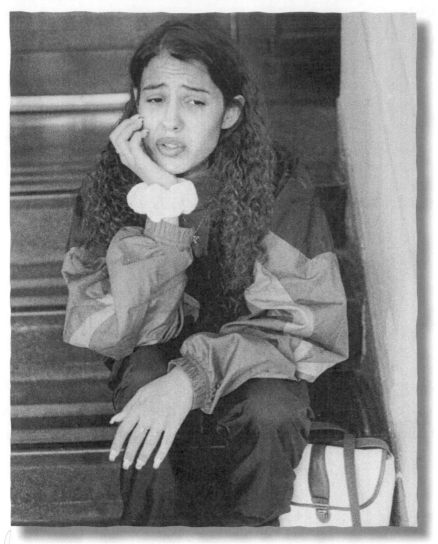

To become a member of the Vice Lords, Kim had to prove herself by fighting five other girls in the gang. "Most of those five were [my] cousins. And they weren't going easy at all on me."

having some really good times. We'd see some gang graffiti from another gang, and we'd cut it out—that means cross it out—and we'd paint up some signs of our own. It was kind of a kick—the thrill of danger, or whatever, the thrill of doing something without getting caught. It was sort of a rush, doing stuff.

"Like when you see some girl and she throws some sign up at you, and it's not your set, and you throw your own sign back up, and she wants to fight. It's a rush. We'd get excited about that—a feeling in the pit of your stomach that kind of tells you that something exciting is going to happen. And part of it was that it was all a secret from my family. I mean, my mom has no idea to this day that I was ever in a gang!

"Now that I'm older, I don't get as worked up about that stuff as I used to. I mean, I have a baby and everything, so maybe that's the reason. I'm not sure. But that isn't to say I can't get into the drama sometimes, you know? I can still fight, like I told you before."

The fights Kim and her cousins were involved with usually started over something minor, she says.

"Oh, it would be a Saturday, and we'd be sitting around on my cousins' front porch," she says. "Let's say a girl walks by. She throws up a sign, to see what I claim, or whatever. Usually, it starts by eye contact. She looks at me and I stare back at her. That tells a lot. So she's wondering what I claim, and then I throw something up.

"Usually it was my cousins who started stuff. I was the quiet one, always watching what was going on. My cousins, though, were obnoxious, always looking to start something, always in your face. That was just their way, I guess. But then once something started, I was in there with them. I didn't back down or nothing."

BEATING UP A QUEEN

Kim recalls one instance where she watched her cousins beat up a girl who was a Queen in the Latin Kings gang.

"She walks right by the house, right by us," she remembers. "She's got the yellow rag on. That's their color. And this girl gives us the eye and throws up an L and a K. And my cousins are right away yelling at her, 'How come you're coming around here, walking by our house? Don't you understand that this is Vice Lords territory? This is west side.'

"And she looks a little scared and starts backing off. And my cousins hop off the porch and walk toward her, throwing the Vice Lords signs. She didn't get away fast enough, 'cause she got beat up good that day. I know, because I was right there, yep.

"Then my two cousins started beating her up, getting real physical. Before that, I mean, it had been just a lot of yelling and cussing. But they busted this girl's head into the curb—stuff like that. I remember thinking to myself, Is she going to go back to her own gang and come back later with more kids to fight with us?

But nothing happened. I mean, she got beat up and bloody and just left.

"What was so stupid about this girl is that she came back other times, too! Each time, she got beat up—sometimes by my cousins, sometimes I'd join in. Eventually my one cousin slashed up her face pretty good, cut her with a razor bade."

ALIAS PEEWEE

As a girl, why did Kim feel it was important for her to engage in violence like that? Isn't beating people up more a tendency of boys than girls? Kim nods, as though she's heard the question a dozen times before.

"See, the reason boys do all this beating up on other people is to get a reputation. It's no different for girls, no different at all. Really, if you want to know the truth, girls need a reputation more, because they seldom get taken seriously.

"Especially me. I mean, I'm so small. It's like people are telling you, 'You can't fight, you can't do this, you can't do that.' I went by the name of Peewee, for obvious reasons. You've got to prove yourself more, especially when you're little like me. Fighting is not just for boys, not at all. I want to be just as hard as the other dudes."

She smiles. "I can fight whoever, and I want to, just to prove that I'm not a little 'wuss.' And I got my butt kicked a couple of times, too. But it was worth it, just for the reputation. Nothing serious, I mean. But black eyes, busted ribs, split lips . . . those kinds of things send a message that you are going to be taken seriously."

Kim says that although she enjoyed the danger of fighting, she would be less than honest if she claimed that she never was afraid.

"I was, really," she says. "I mean, one time I got grazed with a knife, and that scared me. In fact, I think I was more scared *after* the incident was all over, just thinking about it, you know? I had gone with my boyfriend, Petey, to pick up his sister from this one house. Some of the kids at that house didn't want her to go, you know? So they started beating on Petey, who was just trying to protect his sister.

"Well, everyone is joining in, and things are really getting scary, when a knife came out of somebody's pocket. I had jumped in the middle to help Petey, and I saw the knife. I pushed the knife away from Petey, but not until after it sliced my pant leg and scratched

Kim believes that girls need to prove they can fight in order to gain respect from their peers. "Black eyes, busted ribs, split lips . . . those kinds of things send a message that you are going to be taken seriously."

me. The knife ended up cutting the guy who owned it. It cut his hand and arm. Afterwards I couldn't even think about that time without getting really nervous."

"I Couldn't Stop Shaking"

Another time that she still thinks about was when she was on the west side of the city with her cousins, and someone was shooting at them.

"That was closer than I ever want to be," she says, shaking her head. "We were inside the house, and someone was shooting. We didn't see who. The bullet went in the back window and just missed us. You know, I have no idea at all why we were getting shot at. I guess I'm not surprised, with all the stuff me and my cousins got into, but I just didn't expect it to happen like that.

"I'm not really sure why the shooting happened, but I'm pretty sure it was over nothing important. That's what it usually was. Like someone doing the wrong sign, or colors, or someone called someone something, or even stuff like 'you was with my girl.' Stupid things like that, if you really want to know the truth.

"But whatever started it, I don't ever want to be around that kind of fighting again—the bullets whizzing around, the glass inside that house breaking. It was too much. I couldn't stop shaking, couldn't stop crying. And we couldn't call the police. I mean, what would they do? We're in a gang; the shooters were in a gang. What are we going to tell the police anyway?"

Kim says that close calls such as these made her understand one thing about her life: that she was not so reckless as to be unconcerned whether she lived or died.

"I wanted to live," she says emphatically. "I was just saying to myself, 'Let me stay alive now.' I mean, sometimes you hear people say that kids in gangs don't want to live. They hear gangsters say, 'I don't care whether I live or die; it makes absolutely no difference to me.' So other people believe that about all kids in gangs. A stereotype? I don't know. I don't even think it's true any of the time!

"Maybe gangsters think that that kind of attitude makes them harder. I don't know. But I think it's a lie, usually. I think people who say that are fakes. I think most people would be like me if a gun were pointed at them. They don't want to die either. Whatever they're claiming, I don't believe it."

LIVING THE LIFE

Were those days all about fighting? Was that the main activity among young female Vice Lords on the west side of her city? Kim shrugs.

"Kind of, yeah. Well, sometimes it was about making money, I guess. I admit, yeah, I sold drugs sometimes, but not really very often. My cousin did it way more than I did. I didn't want to. I just participated sometimes—sell a couple of eight balls of crack or some weed or something once in a while.

"I'd make a few hundred dollars in a couple of hours, so the money was good. But the stress was awful, not even worth it. I didn't like dealing with the little (geekers) on the street, those crack addicts. They were weird, dirty, and they smelled really bad." She thinks about it a moment and shudders involuntarily. "Ugh, I mean *really* bad.

"We'd walk past each other on the street. I had the stuff in my mouth in a little bag. And we'd walk past each other, and then one of us would go inside a store, or something. The other one would go in a couple minutes later. That's where we'd do the deal, so people wouldn't be as apt to see. No one looked; the addict would just fold the money up real small and hand it to me, right in my palm.

"For an eight ball maybe I'd get twenty dollars. That would be tops. But I could sell quite a few of those in an hour. It was just guys in the neighborhood, so there wasn't a lot of risk. Still, I didn't want to get caught. I had no interest in going off to jail. That would have been terrible."

Kim's voice trails off, as if she is thinking about what jail would have been like. She sighs again and shakes her head.

"So I guess, to be real honest, most of the fun *was* fighting. But don't misunderstand. Me and my cousins were feisty," she says with a hint of pride in her voice. "See, my cousins and me are not just obnoxious to other gangsters and whatever. We all would spend as much time fighting among ourselves as with other people! We were loyal to one another. We'd watch each other's back, but we'd fight each other an awful lot.

"We'd get drunk, start talking to each other, just saying stuff. Hey, once I busted out my cousin's window, got the glass, and tried to stab her with a piece of it! I got a temper, right. It was the same as I was saying before, though: stupid things cause fights. I mean, she said to me, 'I was with your boyfriend last night.' And she sits there smiling at me.

"Well, she's only playing, and I know that. But it just sets me off. So I bust the window, just by throwing something at it. And I tried to stab her. She knew what to say to get me going, and the same with me. A lot of time it was the liquor talking, though."

"SHE WAS SO RUTHLESS"

Almost a gang within a gang, Kim and her cousins continued to fight, both other gangs and one another. Their names were well known on the west side, she says.

"Like I said, I was Peewee, and there was Lorenzo. He was [called] Little Crazy. It seemed like there was nothing he wouldn't do. He was the only one of my cousins that was a boy. And there was Chi Chi. And Gata."

This last name she says quietly, the bravado draining from her voice. "Gata was very special to me," she says. "Her name means 'cat.' She got the name, I think, because of her eyes. They were green, just like cat's eyes. But Gata, she was so tough, she was so ruthless. She was bigger than me, and could she fight! She fought dudes and everything, man. She could fight anybody. Yeah, she carried a pistol.

"Gata was killed two years ago, in October. It was so sad— really hard on her family. See, the family had tried to get away from all the gang stuff by moving down to Texas for a while. They came back after a while and moved into a different neighborhood. Maybe they thought things would be better. I don't really know. But Gata liked to talk, and she wasn't shy about claiming anything. She talked too much, talked a whole bunch of shit."

Drive-by shootings claimed the lives of two of Kim's friends. Though she doesn't know why her friends were shot, she says that most gang violence results from trivial matters.

62

Kim goes on, "So anyway, she was walking to the store one night to get some juice, and on the way back some people did a drive-by and shot her. It was Crips; everyone knew who did it. I mean, the neighborhood was a Crips neighborhood. That's where Gata and her family were living. The police got them, but they got off on a technicality. Anyway, they shot at her head—blew her whole face off."

"REST IN PEACE, GATA"

Kim says that she heard the news from her cousin Lorenzo, who had been the one to find Gata.

"He had heard the shots and went out and found her," she says. "So he found her lying there, and he said that he couldn't even recognize her. He couldn't see a face. He was so upset, Lorenzo was.

"It was hard on me, too," she says, her eyes filling with tears. "The funeral was here, even though the family was originally from Texas. I had to give the eulogy and everything. Boy, that was hard. I cried the whole time I talked. There were lots of people; everyone came. All the Vice Lords wore red. I wore black Dickies and a red shirt that my other cousin had airbrushed. The shirt said 'Rest in Peace, Gata.' It was so cool. I wore a red rag around my head, too."

Kim says that part of the reason it is hard to talk about Gata's death is that Lorenzo recently died, too.

"It was just last summer, on the Fourth of July," she says. "He was up at the park with his little son and Gata's little girl, Dominique. Did I say she had a daughter? Anyway, Dominique was only a year old when Gata was killed.

"So Lorenzo was at the park, and there was a drive-by. He must have heard the car coming, because I guess he jumped on top of his son, who was right next to him. He covered up his son, but he got the bullets himself. They have no idea who did that drive-by, no idea at all. Both the little kids were okay. I guess that's good, at least."

Kim says that Lorenzo's death was ironic, for he was no longer an active Vice Lord.

"He was a victim; I know that," she says. "He had quit gang-banging. He was just taking care of his little boy, since the baby's mother had gone off and left them. The whole thing was stupid. It was stupid for anybody to be shooting, stupid for Lorenzo to die."

And it still makes me so sad that Gata is gone. Her family moved back to Texas, like they did before."

She sighs. "Dominique must be about three now, I guess. I don't even know if I'll ever see [Gata's family] again."

"I SHOULD HAVE KNOWN BETTER"

Does it help relieve some of her sadness now that she has a baby of her own to care for? Kim shrugs.

"I don't know. I was eighteen when I got pregnant, and it's not that I'm with the father of my baby anymore. I have nothing to do with him at all. I met him downtown one day, when I was skipping school. I first saw him there. He seemed real nice. Ronzell—that was his name—he was okay looking . . . good smile and real dark skin. He treated me real polite. We started talking, and then we gradually got to know each other and started going out more.

"But he was a Gangster Disciple," she says with a dismissive wave of her hand. "I should have known better. I should have known he was a GD. I mean, that plaza where I saw him, that's where the GDs hang out."

Are GDs that bad? Kim curls her lip in disdain and shakes her head.

"I hate GDs. They're always causing trouble, always fighting. They're real immature. I mean, they are so stupid the way they set you up. I'll give you an example. Just the other night a bunch of us were at a club, and the GDs started a huge fight. I mean, they're so stupid they were fighting each other. And so everybody gets tossed out of the club; everybody gets in trouble. Set up! I'm serious, that's what they did.

"And the way they talk, it's so stupid. It's like, 'What's up' and 'hey,' and 'Folks this' and 'Folks that.' That's what they call themselves, Folks. I'm so sick of listening to them, really. So it annoys me that I ended up having a baby with one of them."

"HE WANTED A BABY BY ME"

Kim says that although Ronzell's gang status was unknown to her at first, he knew that she was a Vice Lord.

"He didn't make a big deal about it with me," she says. "I don't think he cared all that much one way or another. But I got a lot of mean looks from other Vice Lords, going out with a GD. *Lots* of mean looks. My cousins were the worst. One of them said, 'How are you going to be with us and be seeing someone from another set? How do you think that can happen? You ain't got no respect for us, for your own gang.' Stuff like that. But I guess at first I didn't worry about it. I'm like, 'Whatever.' I thought I was in love, so what I was doing with Ronzell was my business. Like I said before, I don't like people telling me what to do, even if I do care about those people."

Kim says that things seemed to change when she found out she was pregnant.

"My mom and dad were not a problem," she says. "They liked him okay. They don't like him now because of the things he's done recently, such as cheat on me about a million times. He's gotten other girls pregnant. Things like that. But I have to admit, when I found out I was pregnant, I wasn't sure it was his baby at first."

She smiles slightly. "I had cheated on him, yeah. I'd been with this guy Kingston. He was a Crip. And until I had the ultrasound and they had pinpointed the due date, I thought maybe the baby was Kingston's. But it ended up that there was no doubt. It was

Kim got pregnant after she became involved with a boy from another gang. "He wanted a baby by me because he thought us having a kid together would keep me by him."

Ronzell's, and he was happy. He wanted a baby by me because he thought us having a kid together would keep me by him."

"HE'S A LOT OF WORK"

Kim's pregnancy was difficult. After going into premature labor at six months, she was forced to remain in bed for the remainder of her pregnancy.

"I think it was all stress—from the baby's father," she says flatly. "I got to really hate having him anywhere near me, especially after the baby was born. We were fighting quite a bit then, I guess. Anyway, I named the baby Ronzell, after his father. He's fifteen months now, and I wish I hadn't named him that. But it's too late to change it, you know? I mean, he knows his name already, so that would be hard. I call him R. J., though, so it's not so bad, I guess."

Does she enjoy being a mother? Kim sighs and looks off in the distance, as though she is considering her answer very seriously.

"He's cute, R. J. is. But it was so hard at first. He was such a hard baby, so fussy, always screaming and crying all the time. It really got on my nerves. I hated it, back then. My mom helped a lot, I have to admit. I lived with my parents then, just like I do now.

"It was hard for me to get close to him when he was little. I used to ask my parents if they would take the baby, but they said no. But now it's different. I want my baby. He's more interesting, even though he gets into trouble. Like he picks up the phone all the time and starts dialing numbers. But mostly he's fine. He's a lot of work, though, a *lot* of work."

"HE'S JUST STUPID"

Kim says that her relationship with Ronzell was shaky during her pregnancy and deteriorated drastically after R. J.'s birth.

"I can't stand him," she says. "He's just stupid. The gang thing got to be more of a problem, him being a GD and all. He'd always be saying, 'Why don't you be a GD?' and I'd be like, 'Why don't you be a Vice Lord?' And he'd say, 'I don't want to be no Vice Lord,' and I'd be saying, 'Well, I don't want to be no stupid Folk. You're all stupid.' I told him I had no respect for him and his gang. And he'd always be calling me Hook, which is a disrespectful name for a Vice Lord. He'd take my red rag off my head and throw it on the floor. Stuff like that."

Aside from their differences about gangs, Kim says, she has be-

Although she says her baby is becoming easier to care for as he gets older, Kim admits that it is still difficult and challenging to be a young single mother.

come fed up with the fact that Ronzell is sometimes physically abusive to her.

"It started back when I was pregnant, and he heard about maybe I wasn't sure it was his baby," she explains. "He started using his fists on me, hit me in the stomach so I'd lose the baby. Ever since R. J. was born, and Ronzell was in a bad mood, he would start on how it couldn't be his baby, because he is dark skinned and the baby is light skinned. I told him, 'Look, you got a half-brother who is light skinned. It's in your genes.' But he's just stupid, like I said before. It was easier for him to hit me than to think that maybe I was right. I just told him, 'Fine, if you don't want to claim your son, then don't.'

"I don't let him come around anymore, ever since he tried to beat me," she says. "My mouth starts it, I admit. He continually tries to tell me what to do, and I tell him I'm not interested in what he says. I tell him I'll leave him if he keeps ordering me around. And then he gets mad. He backhands me across my face, slaps me. We just start fighting."

Does she ever get tempted to fight back? Kim laughs.

"Fight back? Of course I do! I busted his lip; I hit him in the eye. And he's the reason I don't carry a gun no more. I used to have a little Beretta. But he'd make me so mad all the time, I was afraid I was going to use it on him, so I stopped carrying it. No, Ronzell is not in my life no more—not at all."

Kim says that even though she is not as active in the Vice Lords as she once was, she cannot imagine a time when she would stop claiming the gang.

"It's so important to me," she says. "I mean, it isn't like it was when it was me and my cousins, back in high school. There are other things in my life, too. I mean, back when I was fifteen, being a Vice Lord was a way of life. But even now, I hate the fact that my baby's got a GD father. And one time Ronzell even threw up a GD sign on my baby's chest. I hated that! I told him never, never to do that again."

Does she worry that R. J. might someday want to be in a gang? She shakes her head emphatically.

"No, that wouldn't bother me at all," she declares. "Really. In a way I'd be surprised if he didn't. Look, his cousins are, from his father's side. Their parents are all GDs. The cousins are little, but they already know how to throw up signs. I don't think they know what it means yet, but it ain't long."

She laughs quietly. "I know the first time R. J. does it, it better not be a GD sign, or he'll be getting his hand slapped good. I'd smack him up, I swear. My own cousin has been showing him how to make a Vice Lord sign, and I'm fine with that.

"See, I don't involve my baby with the gang; I don't take him around where he's likely to get hurt. But he's been around it all his life. I dress R. J. in red all the time, and he looks real cute. I put a red rag on him, on his head. That's the way he dresses all the time. I'm not ashamed of that, and I don't want him to be, either."

"I'M SO BORED"

Besides watching her baby grow up, Kim says that she has no great plans for her future. She knows only that at this time she is very bored with her life.

"I am twenty, and me and my baby still live with my parents," she says. "I don't have rules; I can do what I want. I mean, they couldn't control me when I was five, how could they make me do anything now? But I'm so bored—so, so, so bored.

"My mom drives me nuts. She nags. I can't stand being around there. She's in my business all the time. Maybe I'd like to go to Texas, see my relatives there. But maybe just stay here, finish school. I'm a senior, but since I got kicked out of school way back in tenth grade, I'm doing my assignments at home and mailing them in. I just have American history and geometry, I think, and I'm done. But after that, who knows? Maybe something with computers. I'm so sick of my life, it's hard even to think about it."

She looks up suddenly and curls her lip again in disgust.

"Did I say that I think I might be pregnant again? I'm two weeks late, and I'm almost positive. I should buy one of those home tests, but I don't want to face it. I'll go a little longer and just pretend everything is all right."

The father is *not* Ronzell, she says firmly.

"My new boyfriend is in a gang, yeah," she says. "All my boyfriends have been in gangs. This one is a Crip. He's real quiet about it, though. I didn't even guess it until I was snooping around and found out. I'm like, 'You're a Crip?' He's like, 'Yup.' So, I don't know. He knows what I claim, and it isn't an issue with him, not like it was with Ronzell. So maybe things will work out. Who knows?"

STUPID WANNA-BES

Kim reiterates that she is proud of being a Vice Lord but warns that the gang life is not for every girl.

"I'm serious about the fact that it was okay for me," she says. "I don't stand by all the shooting and the killing that people are doing. I think it's stupid, all the fighting about stupid things, and innocent people getting killed.

"But if you're a girl who wants a reputation, if you want people to know you're hard—that you're as hard as any guy—it's the right thing for you. It's just a family. It's people to hang out with, people who will watch your back, and you can watch theirs. For some people who don't have the family they need, their gang is all they know, all they have. It's something just for you, something you have for your own."

Kim curls her lip again.

"There are plenty of little girls out there who get in for the wrong reason, and God, I hate that," she says. "These little wanna-bes who think they're getting into a gang, they want to learn the

Maturity and motherhood have forced Kim to put her fighting days behind her.

signs, wear the colors, hang around the boys. It's so sick.

"I remember in high school . . . the one I went to was so completely white. No gangs at all. This white girl comes up to me one day and calls me a spic or something. So I said, 'Okay, I'll be a spic.' And the next day this girl shows up at school, she's got a red rag on her head. Now remember, I'm in the Vice Lords back in the city with my cousins, so I know all this stuff. I say to her, 'So what do you claim?' She's like, 'I claim Crip.'

"I looked at her a minute. I say, 'Well, you got the wrong color on your head.' I ripped that red rag right off her head. I say, 'Don't be wearing my color.' We got in a fight for that, but I won. And there was no way I would lose a fight to a stupid wanna-be like that. There's too many of them around."

Kim smiles.

"I got a temper, like I say. There aren't too many fights anymore, but I'm not walking away from them all. But like I told you, I don't carry my gun no more. And lately, I've even stopped carrying a knife. I put it away because I almost stabbed my boyfriend the other day. Putting it away seemed like the best idea."

Dewayne

"I'LL ALWAYS THINK OF MYSELF
AS A CRIP. . . . I'D TEAR
SOMEBODY UP IF I WAS BEING
THREATENED. . . . BUT THE
DIFFERENCE NOW IS I DON'T
WANT TO LOSE MY LIFE OVER NO
NONSENSE."

One wouldn't know he was blind at first. A tall, rangy young man of eighteen, Dewayne moves quickly through the dining room into the living room of his mother's house. He has no difficulty maneuvering around the table until he bumps up against a dining room chair, left out by one of his younger sisters.

"Who left this out here?" he booms in a resonating bass. "I can't be finding my way through here if you all are leaving chairs everywhere."

He continues his walk into the room and offers his hand in the direction of his visitor's voice. As he begins to introduce himself, a young-looking woman in orange leggings and a yellow blouse rushes in from the kitchen.

"I'm so glad you could come," she says, smiling brilliantly at the visitor. "I'm his mother, Ann. I'm very proud that Dewayne here is going to be in a book. I think there is so much he can do for other young people out there, am I right? He's been through so much, so much. Am I right, Dewayne?"

Without even acknowledging her, Dewayne sinks down into the soft cushions of the sofa. He begins to speak.

"I'm totally blind," he says in his deep, lilting bass, which is almost mesmerizing in its rhythm. "I can't see nothing—no light, no anything. I been like this since December 14, 1994. That's when I got shot.

"What happened was, I was up in Curly's Cafe, and I saw someone looking in the window at me. I knew the dudes. I didn't associate with them, you understand, but I knew them. See, I was a Crip, and these guys were Crips, too, only not the same set. It's not like some thing in the old movies, how everybody is like brothers in the gang. See, every gang has different sets, different branches. And the Crips are huge, man. So there are lots of different sets, lots of them.

"Anyway, when I stepped outside, the one guy I knew said 'What's up' back to me. The other guy, the one who ended up shooting me, he gave me a real funny look. And we just started walking a little bit, when I saw, out of the corner of my eye, the guy pull out a gun. So I tried to run. I made it across the street, but that's all I remember. I don't really know what happened after that, except when I woke up a long time later, I was in the hospital. I had my eyes all bandaged, and I could hear my mom talking."

"I Remember Plenty"

"Well, I remember lots more than that," says his mother, who had been standing in the adjoining room listening. "I remember plenty, in fact. I remember when somebody was doing that to my son, taking away his sight for the rest of his life, I was at home. I was trying to get ready for a birthday party for my younger son.

"Then the telephone rang, and it's the medical center downtown, asking if I was Dewayne's mother. I heard that man identify himself, and I thought, oh please, God, no. I told the man, 'No, no, no, no I don't want to hear it! I don't want to hear it!' I had just come from the grocery store and I was running water for a bath. I said, 'Nope, please don't tell me!'"

Ann shakes her head and closes her eyes, trying to hold back a sob.

"I have to say that man respected me enough to call one of my sisters who lives near here. And she came over and said, 'Let's go—this, that, and the other has happened to your kid—let's go.' So that's how it happened."

Dewayne starts to speak, but she starts in again: "We went to the hospital, and they told me, 'Hey, he might not make it. The next two hours are crucial. He may not come out of this.' But you know what I felt like? I felt like they already believed he was going to die, because they had a toe tag on him! Truly, they had his toe tagged, and homicide was there, wanting to ask me questions about Dewayne and what might have happened to him.

"They were sure he would die," she says, her voice rising, "but my faith was so strong. I believe in Jesus, you see, and I know what God can do. I was afraid, but I prayed, and that's why my son lived. I know that. I mean, he was on his deathbed—his *deathbed*! But look at him now! The only thing he can't do is see."

A SIGN

Dewayne has been sitting quietly but now rejoins the conversation.

"I got shot in the left side of my head," he explains, "but the bullet destroyed my right eye. It was shot out. I got shot in my side first; that shot got me down. But then the dude came over and shot me in the head."

"Yeah," his mother says with a nod. "They told me at the hospital that they removed one eye at the scene because they were going to try to save the other eye. Yes, they removed it, took it out. But the fragments of the bullet, when it exploded, were so powerful that they destroyed the nerves and everything, so they couldn't even save that other eye. They got most of the fragments out, but they said there were still some in there."

"You ask me why they shot me," Dewayne says. "Hey, one of the things I've asked myself a million times since that day is why they shot me. I do it over and over in my mind. I ain't never done nothing to either one of them guys. I just don't know for certain."

"You know," his mother interrupts, "there was a sign that day, when I was in the grocery store. I thought about Dewayne, just thought about him. And I got home, and my younger son says, 'Mama, Dewayne called, and he says call him back [on his pager]. He wants to come home.' So then I thought, I'll just take my bath and call him. It was a sign, but I didn't listen right, I guess. And right after that, the hospital called."

GANG RELATED

Dewayne had been fidgeting impatiently while his mother talked, but at the mention of a sign, he nods his head.

"Yeah, I felt something too, before it happened. Before it had all happened, I just felt something was going to happen to me. I

Looking back, both Dewayne and his mother say they ignored warning signs that something was wrong on the day Dewayne was shot by gang members.

had got into it with some Vice Lords. Nothing came of it, but I remember that afterwards I felt kind of shady, you know? I kept looking out the alley, looking at them, wondering if something else was going to happen to me that day. I was nervous, yeah, feeling shady.

"I called my mom, 'cause I just felt that feeling. She wasn't there. I told my brother to tell her I wanted to come home, that she should just call my pager. I'd lay low for a while, come home, hang around here alone, and just be quiet, you know?"

Now it is his mother's turn to be impatient. She waves her hand in the air, as if trying to sweep away his words.

"Now, Dewayne, what you're saying is new to me, brand new. You're talking just like them police that came to the hospital. They write in their notebook, 'Gang related,' and they leave it at that. They just go on, shrug their shoulders, and act like, well, that's the answer. It's gang related. So what does that mean? I ask you Dewayne, what does that mean, gang related?"

She wipes tears away from her cheeks and continues. "I don't believe you was in that gang, Dewayne. I refuse to believe that. Re*fuse*. Do you hear me? You can say it all you want, but I refuse. I don't believe it." Dewayne shakes his head impatiently. "Yeah, Mom, whatever. It *was* gang related. I was in the gang."

He pauses, as his mother continues to talk. "Oh my goodness." "Mom." "My goodness." "Will you please listen? Mom, that's what I'm telling you. I'm telling you the shooting was gang related. Now just stop talking, and listen to what *I* got to say, okay? Just listen!"

Ann sits down on the dining room chair that Dewayne had stumbled over earlier.

"Yes, I'm sorry. Go on," she says softly. "I'm listening."

THE SHADY DAY

"What I was saying," Dewayne insists, "was that the day seemed shady to me, like there was something that was going on. Like I said, I'd had a run-in with these Vice Lords down on Lake Street at a center there. It's usually cool there, even though the Vice Lords hang out there a lot, 'cause it's open—people going in and out all the time.

"So I was in there with some of my boys, you know, shooting some pool and playing video games. And one of them Vice Lords comes up to me, and he like threatened me, out of his mouth. It wasn't so much the words, but it was, you know, like how he was speaking to me. He was like, 'What you rab-ass niggers doing in here?' I was like, 'What?'

"I dropped what I was eating, my pop and my potato chips, right on the ground. And my boys just jumped off their video games, and some of his boys come over. I wasn't scared, just excited. That's the way it always was for me, back when I was an active Crip, you know. When stuff like that happens, it's just a rush, like something's going to happen and you're going to be involved.

"Anyway, a few of us had pistols on us. We walked outside and just were standing around, you know, just talking and stuff back and forth. Nothing really materialized, you know? So we just maintained, just walked down the street, me and my boys. We went over to one of their houses, and we were talking about what we were going to do about this. We knew we had to prepare, so three of my friends went down a few blocks to buy some more bullets."

Dewayne remembers that he decided to kill some time while he was waiting for them by going to Curly's Cafe.

"Like I said, I felt real shady, so I decided to call my mom," he says. "I'd go home and hang out, then maybe find those Vice Lords later on. But then, I saw this one dude that I knew from a long time back. We were cool even though he's a Blood. But he didn't represent himself to me that way, you know? We was just people. We was just talking about this and that."

"I NEVER TURNED HIM IN"

Dewayne says that as he and the Blood gang member were talking, a car pulled up with several Crips in it.

"This is the whole reason I got shot, I think," he says. "I mean, I thought about it, and this is what I think. I mean, the one dude that went to get the ammunition? He's with these other guys I don't know; one of them later shot me. Anyway, the one I knew says 'What's up?' to me, kind of surprised-like, like, why am I talking to a Blood? Just 'What's up?'

"That made me real paranoid," he muses aloud. "Like, why wouldn't he say anything else? I don't know . . . that bothered me a lot. So anyway, the car pulls away. I just kept talking a minute or two, and then I went inside. And later—well, you know what happened."

Dewayne says that he has since run into the person who shot him, even though he can get no definitive explanations from fellow Crips about what happened that day.

"What I'm hearing is that he didn't know I was a Crip, that maybe because I was talking to a Blood, he thought I was a Blood, too," he says. "I mean, I was wearing a blue rag, and he's telling his friends he couldn't tell I was a Crip. I don't think so. Well anyway, he's still a little shady on me 'cause he popped me, and he knows I still got my brain, and I'm still walking around knowing he's the one who did it.

"I never turned him in, no. I never did, 'cause when I was first in the hospital, I was so afraid. I was paranoid, thinking, okay, if I turn him in, some of his boys from his same set are going to come in here and finish me off. And I was hearing about my mom going around trying to find out who did it, asking my friends if they

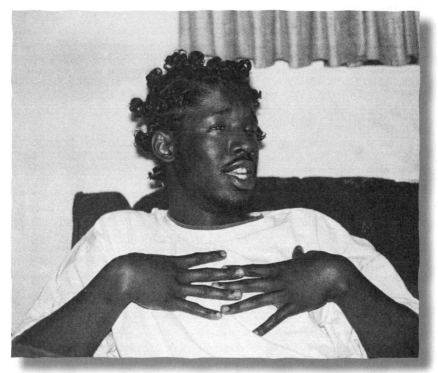

Though Dewayne knows who shot him, he has never turned in the shooter or confronted him. "He's still a little shady on me 'cause he popped me, and he knows I still got my brain."

know who the shooter was. They was talking to homicide detectives and everything, telling them not to stop looking for the guy. And that made me nervous, too, because I love my mom, and I don't want my mom to get hurt. I told her not to do anything like that and that I wasn't going to tell the police anything."

"I WAS THE ONLY ONE WHO CARED"

Ann has jumped to her feet, unable to listen any further. "He knew, he knew who had done this to him," she wails. "But he refused to tell the police. And I feel that when somebody does somebody bodily harm, deprives them of their sight like they did to him, it's a duty to bring that person to justice. That boy that done this? He's got no rights. He gave them up when he pulled that trigger.

"Listen, I struggled with the streets. I didn't know where I was. I was in bad neighborhoods, but I didn't care; I wanted answers. I was the only one who cared, I think. I mean, the police . . . they were no good. They closed the case; I had to force them to reopen it.

See, Dewayne was a young black male, and that means they can treat him like just another statistic. Gang related! See what I mean?"

She pounds her fist on the wall. "No, no, no! They never called me; I called them to see if they had leads. I talked to supervisors, sergeants, whatever. No one had anything new, no one was working on anything. No leads, no leads. Just because they labeled it gang related. So what do they do? They close the case."

Her voice is deep with emotion. "Listen. I am this way: I love the children of the world. They have no color as far as I am concerned. I think everybody needs to work harder, do their job, so the children of the world are safe, so they don't get labeled and thrown away. That's the way I am, that's the way I was brought up back in Mississippi. Love all the children, not just the ones in your family.

"Like once, my Dewayne got in some trouble. His parole officer told him he had to be in school from now on, real regular. And then, when Dewayne started not going to school again, I called that man, told him that Dewayne wasn't fulfilling his obligation. And you know what he said to me? He said, 'What am I supposed to do about that?'"

WHOSE FAULT?

Ann shakes her head sadly. "It makes me so angry that people blame these kids, when we are failing them every day. Where are the parole officers, the judges, the police, the counselors? Where were they all when my Dewayne got his sight taken?"

"Mom, Mom!" Dewayne thunders. "Listen, Mom, will you please listen to me for a minute? It was *my* decision; I was living my life. Don't act like it was somebody else's fault. I was the one who was carrying that pistol. I was the one looking for trouble. No one made me do those things. Why you acting like somebody else is controlling me?"

"It was not your fault, Dewayne!" his mother shrieks. "Not your fault *at all*! It was just like that one white boy who killed that policeman a couple weeks ago. I heard his mother on television. She was saying, 'I went through the system, and the system denied my kid. And now they got him for killing a police officer.' That's the way I feel, Dewayne, like the system denied you."

He groans, shaking his head back and forth. "Mom, that's how life *is*. Why can't you understand that? That white boy that killed that police officer has to take responsibility for what he did, same as me. I mean . . . oh, Mom, what are you saying? You ain't even making sense!"

"And like that boy who killed that lady and her baby when he was robbing them," Ann continues, as if Dewayne hadn't spoken. "He had been in the system before; he'd been arrested. And what had the system done for him? They failed him, that's what. I don't condone what he did, I know that. But what about the people that knew he was capable of that? Same with my kid. The system knew he was going to be in trouble, so why didn't they do something? You were on probation, but they didn't hold you to anything. That parole officer didn't do his job. I called that parole officer when you got shot, Dewayne. I told him, 'You failed my son.'"

"INTO THE STORM"

By now Dewayne is completely frustrated. As his mother talks, he mutters and shakes his head. At the thought of his mother's accusing his parole officer of being responsible for his being shot, he explodes.

"Mom!" he says in disbelief. "My goodness! What are you saying? I failed myself, Mom. Why you blaming other people? I failed myself. I got to live my life the way I do. Nobody can make me do things. I make mistakes, I do it wrong sometimes. That jail, that counseling that happened a long time ago—I did all that, but when I got out, I decided I still wanted to do the other stuff, you know? *I* made the decision! *I* violated probation! *I* did that!"

"But they didn't make you better, Dewayne," his mother insists. "They should have taken you back there, made you go to some other school, kept you out of trouble."

"Mom, the system didn't do anything for me because I didn't want it to back then," he argues. "The system didn't do nothing but make me act harder. That's what I said. I ruined things for myself. Even if they'd been tougher on me, I would still have been out there acting hard, acting bad, maybe even be dead by now.

"I didn't join no gang because somebody scared me into it, Mom, or because they made me. No, because *I* wanted to, that's why. That's what you got to be hearing. Just 'cause you make plans for me doesn't mean I always follow them."

Ann is still unconvinced. "I struggled, growing up down in Mississippi. But I had two parents who loved me. We worked together, we believed in God, and we knew things would get better.

At a certain age, as long as you're not stupid and you can under-stand the language in our society, you make your own choices. And I did, Dewayne. I made the right choices.

"And that's what I want for you. I want you to make the right choices, too. I want you to get through the storm, not be caught up in the storm, Dewayne. I did what I could, what I can for you, for all seven of your brothers and sisters. But you went into the storm, De-wayne, and I told you, 'No, don't go there.' But you didn't listen."

A DIFFERENT WORLD

At this she begins to cry, covering her eyes with the palms of her hands.

"Mom, I know I did," says Dewayne, trying to be more gentle. "I know you wanted the best for me, and I know you warned me about the trouble I was headed for. But that was the choice I made. Not you. I followed my friends, did what I thought would be more exciting for me. I went that direction. I didn't want to fol-low your rules, remember? That's why I left, that's why I started running away when I was twelve. Because I didn't want to follow your rules."

Dewayne believes he is responsible for his own actions: "I didn't join no gang because somebody scared me into it. No, because I wanted to, that's why."

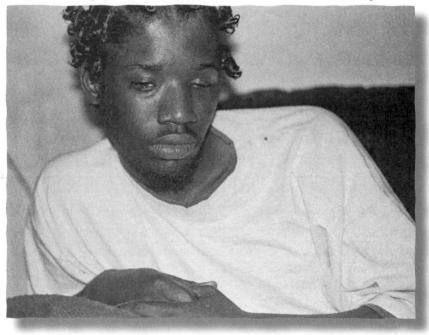

Ann sniffs. "Dewayne, I know how life is. I grew up———"

"Mom," he interrupts, "you grew up in another time. It was a different world. You don't know how life is now. This is the nineties. You're from Jackson, Mississippi, from a long time ago. This is life now. Kids don't listen to their parents, and they don't do things they're supposed to. Like I tell you with my little brothers Dominic and Miguel. You're their mother; they listen to you. But they still are going to do what they want. Am I right?"

"I don't want them to do those things, Dewayne," his mother begins.

"I know, but they do them anyway," he says. "Am I right?"

Ann seems defeated now. "I can't help. I want good for my children. I give them a good home, a good foundation. Then I feel guilty because I don't go to pick Dewayne up. I run bath water."

She begins to cry again. "I want you to have a high school education, graduate. Same with the others. That's my plan for all of you kids. Before I die, I want to know that you're going to be okay. I want you to learn things you need to know: the texture of money, how to read your mail. I don't want nobody putting my kid in a nursing home. I worry about things like that. I want you to go on, be somebody. Life is a struggle, but for you, Dewayne, you got to struggle harder. You got to promise me."

Dewayne nods resignedly. "I am going to learn those things, Mom. And I know life is a struggle. But I can't learn those things just for you, Mom. Don't say it like that. I love you. You know that. You're my mom. But I got to do these things because I need to, for me, because it's right for me."

He moves his hands forcefully across the air in front of him, as though erasing the conversation.

"Man, I got to get outside or something. I can't do this no more, Mom. Back away, please."

IN TROUBLE EARLY

Ann walks past Dewayne, patting his shoulder as she heads back to the kitchen. It is clear that the discussion is not over, that the topic will arise again between them.

"I do love my mom," he says. "It's just so hard all the time. I think she feels guilty about my getting hurt, like I'm blaming her. And that's silly, because how could I do that?

"You ask me when I started with the Crips in the first place. I'll

81

tell you. I've been in trouble since I was about twelve years old. Like I said before, I started taking off from here, going off with my friends when I was twelve or so. I didn't like my mom telling me I had to be in at a certain time or that I had to do homework, or whatever. Just rules, and I didn't want them.

"So I got in trouble," he says. "Bad trouble, some of it. Some of it I don't even want to talk about, okay? I'll tell you one thing. Me and my friends were with some older girls once, walking them home. And they got raped by some guys we knew. These guys had followed us 'cause they saw the girls. They ended up raping them in an abandoned house. Me and my friends, we had nothing to do with the rape, but we got questioned.

"They ended up catching three of the dudes that did it, but I don't think they caught them all. The girls explained about us to the police, though, so it got sorted out. But after that, I guess I started getting in worse trouble.

"When I was fourteen, I shot someone." Dewayne is visibly uncomfortable with this topic. "I hurt him real bad, real bad. I had chased him for a while. He was a kid, yeah, about my age. The police found out and arrested me. I got sent to jail, spent some time there, and then went to a county home school for a while. I was in that system about a year and a half, locked up.

"When I got out of there, I was about fifteen," he continues. "I had gotten into fights with people in jail and stuff, or in group homes, or whatever. I kept on violating what I was supposed to do, so I'd get put back in. It just kept going on. I was bad then. I used to drag people out of their cars, beat them up. I had a pistol. Hey, I had my first pistol when I was twelve."

WHY THE CRIPS?

Dewayne says that as a young kid in trouble and in the system, it was more important than ever to have a gang affiliation.

"You had to have a reputation," he says. "Especially in jail. You got to have respect there—just like out on the streets, in your 'hood—or you are a dead man. You can't count on nobody; that's a fact. So you got to prove not only that you're hard as an individual, but that you are connected. You know what I'm saying?

"Now, when I was younger, I hung around a lot with GDs because my cousins and my uncles were GDs. They kept trying to get me in their shoes, claim the GDs, but I didn't want to be in no gang back then. I got to the age of fourteen, though, and I had to decide. I decided to claim the Crips. I had some friends that were Crips, and that's what I decided then."

Has he ever reconsidered his decision? Dewayne smiles.

"That's a tough question, with two answers. I mean, I've asked myself why I got put in one category, which I now think was the wrong move for me. I have associates that are Bloods, GDs, Vice

Holding the cane he now uses to get around, Dewayne poses with a friend in front of his mother's house.

Lords. Even Bloods, like I said before, and they are the biggest rival of the Crips. My Crips didn't like that. They didn't want me associating with no other gangs.

"But I'm not sorry I chose Crips. I'm still a Crip, still true. In fact, I'll always think of myself as a Crip. I love blue, you know. I'd tear somebody up if I was being threatened. I'd find a way to do that even without my sight. But the difference now is I don't want to lose my life over no nonsense. That's the trouble today, I think. There are a few Crips today I'm still true to. But there's a lot of phony ones around here. Too much infighting, you understand? Too much running around with their little homies, making up their own rules, their own wars."

"No Loyalty"

Dewayne is disgusted by the number of new branches of gangs. Many of these, he says, are run by virtual newcomers.

"See, there's a definite organization to a gang," he explains. "You start out as a soldier—no rank. You just are there to do what the older people tell you. Then as you grow, you accomplish things in the gang, so you get promoted. There's BGs, baby gangsters. And then Gs, gangsters. That's what I was. And finally there are OGs. They are the ones that have been in a long time, who are the organizers. They run things, make the decisions.

"But in all these damn gangs now, in all these new little sets, they got Gs running them," he says. "They're busy ordering everybody around, representing themselves as OGs, when they ain't. They tell people to do this or do that or tell people to go make money a certain way. That's completely wrong, man. Completely. And with all the sets, there is no loyalty to the main gang. Grape Street Crips, Shotgun Crips. Some wear purple, some brown. New sets all the time. Nobody is remembering that they are first *Crips*, you know what I'm saying?"

Dewayne insists that people need to understand that much of the violence associated with gangs is because of how these new sets carry themselves.

"It's absolutely true," he says. "Not just Crips, but everybody. Well, maybe not Bloods; they got their gang to be tight. They are united, they are together. I got to give them credit for that. But the rest of them, including mine, it ain't like that. If it's going to be a gang, then you tell me: why are they acting like they are, shooting at other people in their own gangs, popping innocent people like they be doing?

"Everybody can't just go around doing their own style. It ain't like that, with the same 'hood against each other. That's just how it is. That's what I call phony people. They just are getting into gangs so they can be known. They ain't caring about their 'hood, about their own people. They don't even know what their 'hood is about, you know? That's phony. I hate that."

DOING DRAMA

While Dewayne maintains that he did nothing to undermine his gang, he admits that he participated in his share of what he calls drama.

"Yeah, there were lots of times I was into danger," he says. "I shot at people, got shot at. Like once, I saw a guy who I knew was trying to get me. I saw him walking down a quiet street, and I knew I had to get him first, to show him what I was about. So I ran up on him, shot at the dude. Didn't hit him though.

"Another time, at Curly's, he came up on me. He sat there, showing me this big old gun he had. Just pulled it out of the waistband of his pants. He said to me, 'What's up?' I said, 'What's up?' My boys saw what was happening, and they ran to get me another strap [gun]. And the two of us went outside, parlayed from there, just talked. Lots of talk back and forth, showing guns at each other. See, that's what it was about sometimes. Just making sure each of you knew what was the possibility."

What about police? Did he have much trouble once he was let out of jail? Dewayne shakes his head.

"Nah. I never had too much trouble with them. See, I was never a real obvious person after the age of about fifteen. I didn't go around claiming things, being all public. That's just foolishness, like I told you. That's what these other little dudes and their brand new sets are doing. Myself, I'd creep, just do things on my own, quietly. I made my own money my own way. I'd rob people, whatever. I did that on my own. Didn't do things with other people, usually. And I'd sell drugs. My mom never knew that, but I had to have some money, you know?"

Today, says Dewayne, his life is definitely undramatic. Although he will always consider himself a Crip, he is in name only.

One of Dewayne's younger siblings looks on as he recounts his days with the Crips. Although he still proudly calls himself a Crip, he is no longer active with the gang and forbids his younger brothers to join a gang: "You ain't never going to be in a gang, not while I'm breathing."

"I'm not active no more," he says simply. "I still hang out with people in the same 'hood; I still sit in their apartments, chilling with them. But I can't do no drama like they are doing now. And that nonsense about how you can't get out of a gang once you're in? That's a lie. That just came out of somebody's mouth, but it ain't the truth.

"Maybe it's that way back in California or something. I don't know. But around here, nobody cares. It's an inconvenience, that's all. I mean, it's all about exploiting people. They use the younger ones to do their business, make their money, sell their drugs, drive by, and hurt the people that are their enemies, or whatever. But they can always get more of the young ones who will be happy to do that stuff, true indeed."

He smiles, as if catching himself in self-contradiction.

"It's like my brother Miguel. He's fifteen. He's been in some trouble, but now he's doing good—got a job and everything. He was on the edge of a gang, you know? Trying to follow in his big brother's footsteps. I told him and my other brother, 'You ain't never going to be in a gang, not while I'm breathing.' I feel very strongly about that, yes, indeed.

"But I also feel that there are always going to be gangs. You can't stop them. Gang is like family: you need your associates around you, shoot some dice, smoke some weed. It gives you a family. Hang out, this and that. It helps you feel comfortable."

"I DIDN'T NEED TO BE RUTHLESS"

But what about those young people who come from strong families, families with values like his own family's? Dewayne pauses a moment.

"I guess it's possible not to need a gang. I'm not saying my own family wasn't strong. Maybe I wasn't, I don't know. But it's possible. Now, looking back, I'm sure I wouldn't have stayed with it. Gangbanging is behind me now. It should have been behind me a long time ago.

"See, the thing is that you should be able to outgrow it real quick. Me, I just had to show myself, prove to myself that I was that Crip that I wanted to be. I don't even know why I stayed with it, but I'll tell you truly that I wish I hadn't.

"I like being around lots of people, whatever their 'hood. I can make friends without checking out somebody's rag to see if it's the right color, if I'm allowed to talk to them. I could be friends with those Bloods, or whoever. I wish I'd done that: hung around with people that were enjoyable to me and not worried about their 'hood. I didn't need to be ruthless. That shouldn't have been important."

Dewayne smiles ruefully. "But a lot of things seem clearer now that I'm not in the middle of them, you know? I think that's the way it always is."

"I KNOW THERE'S A LORD"

He is unsure about many things in his life now, he says, and that makes it hard to be around his family. He's got an apartment of his own on the other side of town, so he can be as independent as he wants to be.

"I know I make my mom mad sometimes," he says. "But she just don't understand how things are nowadays. I know she tries because she loves all us kids. But sometimes we do things that disappoint her, and that's life, I guess.

"She's real religious, and that's a help to her. I'm not that way, though. I listen to what my mom says about things, yeah. I respect what she believes, but I think . . . I think that life is just what it is, you know? You just got to live it the way it comes to you. You got to go day by day.

"I know there's a Lord. That much I really believe. I know I don't want to have no pains whenever I do rest in peace. Whichever way it is, heaven or hell, I guess I'll find out when the time comes. I sure do hope it ain't for some time yet, though."

Dewayne says that he hates the part of religion that is quick to condemn things as evil or wicked.

"I think that's all a mistake," he says. "I mean, it's evil to kill people, to steal things that aren't your own. It's evil to disrespect your parents. That kind of stuff, true indeed. But what about certain plants—why are they illegal? If the Lord made it, like weed, man, you can't tell me it's wicked. It should just be there, I think. Just 'cause it gives somebody a good feeling in their brain, so what? It's just the system—the religion, the politics, whatever. That's who's messing things up, confusing things."

Dewayne knows that his behavior sometimes upsets his mother. "But," he says, "she just don't understand how things are nowadays."

MAYBES

While his mother would like him to promise certain things about his future, Dewayne insists that there is no way he can at this point. He has no clear idea of where he is going.

"I know I need to get a diploma," he says. "I mean, I don't want to go through my life not having graduated from high school. I know that much. But whether I'll go back to school or do a GED type of thing, I'm not sure right now. It's hard for me, not being sure—harder on me than it is for my mom. She don't know that, though.

"See, she don't understand that, that I need to know what I'm doing before I do it. I don't want to just start some program or something just because she thinks it's a good plan for me. I'll fail, that way, sure enough. I need to know so I got energy for doing that thing, so I'll do a good job at it. That way, while I'm doing it and it gets hard or boring, then I can just remember why I decided to do it in the first place, not just because everybody told me to.

"I've always wanted to be a rapper," he says, a little self-consciously. "I wanted to go somewhere where there was a big recording studio, record companies. I think that would be good. But now, when I try rapping with some of my friends, I get frustrated trying to remember the raps since I can't write them down.

Dewayne sighs. "My mom pins this stuff on me, these hopes she has. I first got to get better at just managing myself day to day. I been to the Institute for the Blind, so I learned some Braille, learned to move around on my own, use a cane."

He reaches down to the floor next to him, and picks up a folded white cane. "I use this, and I'm getting real good with it. Maybe sometime I'll get me a seeing-eye dog. I think that would be cool. But you know, that's a commitment. I got to be as trained as that dog."

He leans forward, and talks in a softer voice.

"See, before I can go anywhere, I feel like there's something that's freezing me in one place now. I've got to get over it, I know. It's just that I have these dreams: I keep running into the dude that shot me. And in my dreams, I'm having revenge. They're those kind of dreams. I've got a gun in my hand, and I'm chasing him, creeping him, sneaking around, whatever. I'm where he is. That spooks me, you know? I got to get beyond those dreams, or I'll never get anywhere."

Epilogue

Since their first interviews, the four young people in this book have experienced some changes in their lives.

As *The Other America: Gangs* goes to press, Tajan is still active in the Gangster Disciples. He spent a month this summer in California staying with relatives—a trip he says he really enjoyed. He recently bought a tan 1983 Cadillac, which he spends time working on in his backyard. He has quit his job at the pizza place, and when asked how he affords his car payments and insurance he just shrugs. "Just lucky," he says, smiling.

As she suspected when she was first interviewed, Kim is indeed pregnant. Her baby is due in mid-April 1997. She says that her boyfriend is not pleased about the baby. She feels tired and out of sorts most of the time, although her doctors have told her that everything is going well. She and her son continue to live with her parents.

Dewayne has broken up with his girlfriend, and says he is not dating anyone now. He has recently toured a school for the blind in the southern part of the state, and is awaiting information about scholarships.

Edwin's mother, Marta, says that he has moved back to El Salvador. "He wasn't happy at all lately, and he was worried about all the stuff his gang friends were getting into," she says. Marta says, too, that Edwin was increasingly frustrated and angry at home, especially with the rules and guidelines that she set. "I'd tell him to be in by 10:00 at night, and he'd come in at 4:00 in the morning," she says. "He'd get angry with me for scolding him; he'd kick the door and throw things. It's probably better that he left. At least I know he's with my sister and her family, so he's being taken care of. And I know he'll come back when he's 18, and not underage anymore."

Places to Write for More Information

Guardian Angels
982 E. 89th St.
Brooklyn, NY 11236

Dedicated to taking back the streets from gangs and other criminals, the Guardian Angels have information on how citizens can make a difference in wiping out gang activity.

National School Safety Center
4165 Thousand Oaks Blvd., Suite 290
Westlake, CA 91362

This agency concerns itself primarily with the issues of gangs within schools and provides speakers and written material offering suggestions on making our schools safer.

National Urban League
500 E. 62nd St.
New York, NY 10002

The National Urban League offers written materials that show the toll gang activity takes on cities. The league also provides some constructive ways for families and businesses to reclaim the cities of America.

National Youth Gang Information Center
4301 Fairfax Dr., Suite 730
Arlington, VA 22203

This organization is sponsored by the U.S. Department of Justice and distributes information about a wide variety of gang-related subjects.

For Further Reading

Mark S. Dunston, *Street Signs: An Identification Guide of Symbols of Crime and Violence*. Powers Lake, WI: Performance Dimension Publishing, 1992. A very usable guide to understanding and identifying gang signs.

Sandra Gardner, *Street Gangs in America*. New York: Franklin Watts, 1992. Well written, with a good section on the history of street gangs.

Debra Goldentyer, *Gangs*. Austin, TX: Raintree Steck-Vaughn Publishers, 1994. Excellent section on drugs and gangs.

Dan Korem, *Suburban Gangs: The Affluent Rebels*. Richardson, TX: International Focus Press, 1994. Very readable book, which shows the movement of the street-gang mentality to wealthy suburbs across America.

Karen Osman, *Gangs*. San Diego, CA: Lucent Books, 1992. An easy-to-read overview of gangs. Includes a glossary and index.

Marilyn Tower Oliver, *Gangs: Trouble in the Streets*. Springfield, NJ: Enslow Publishing, 1995. Helpful glossary and index.

Margot Webb, *Coping with Street Gangs*. New York: Rosen Publishing, 1991. Excellent section in back of book listing phone numbers to call for teens in gangs or anyone with concerns.

Index

ABOUT THE AUTHOR

Gail B. Stewart is the author of more than eighty books for children and young adults. She lives in Minneapolis, Minnesota, with her husband, Carl, and their sons, Ted, Elliot, and Flynn. When she is not writing, she spends her time reading, walking, and watching her sons play soccer.

Although she has enjoyed working on each of her books, she says that *The Other America* series has been especially gratifying. "So many of my past books have involved extensive research," she says, "but most of it has been library work—journals, magazines, books. But for these books, the main research has been very human. Spending the day with a little girl who has AIDS, or having lunch in a soup kitchen with a homeless man—these kinds of things give you insight that a library alone just can't match."

Stewart hopes that readers of this series will experience some of the same insights and perhaps better understand someone of the Other America.

ABOUT THE PHOTOGRAPHER

Twenty-two-year-old Natasha Frost has been a photographer for the *Minnesota Daily*, the University of Minnesota's student newspaper, for three and a half years. She currently attends the University of Minnesota and is studying sociology and journalism.

When not working at the paper or going to school, Frost enjoys traveling. "It gives me a chance to meet different people and expand my knowledge about the world."

LINCOLN HEIGHTS